Forbidden Images

Forbidden Images

The Secrets of the Tarot

David LeMieux

BARNES & NOBLE BOOKS

A DIVISION OF HARPER & ROW, PUBLISHERS

New York, Cambridge, Philadelphia, San Francisco
London, Mexico City, São Paulo, Singapore, Sydney

FIRST EDITION

Designer: Gilda Hannah

Library of Congress Cataloging in Publication Data

LeMieux, David.
   Forbidden images.

   1. Tarot. I. Title.
BF1879.T2L43   1985   133.3'2424   84-47585
ISBN 0-06-464092-2

85 86 87 88 89 10 9 8 7 6 5 4 3 2 1

To My Parents

*And to my Friends and Acquaintances at the
Holyoke Center in Cambridge, Massachusetts*

Et in Arcadia Ego
(A Secret Anagram on a Painting by Poussin)

Contents

Acknowledgments

I'd like to thank the following authors and their publishers for providing me with important information related to the subject of Tarot symbolism.

To Mouni Sadhu, author of *The Tarot,* and to Dr. Gerard Encausse (Papus), author of *The Tarot of the Bohemians.* Both published by Wilshire Books of Los Angeles.

To Irving Friedman, author of *Book of Creation,* and to Eliphas Levi, author of *The History of Magic.* Both published by Samuel Weiser of New York.

To Alice Hutton, author of *The Cards Can't Lie,* published by Jupiter Books, London.

To Elaine Pagels, Ph.D., author of *The Gnostic Gospels,* published by Random House, New York.

To Joseph Campbell, Ph.D., and Richard Roberts, authors of *Tarot Revelations,* published by Vernal Equinox Press, San Anselmo, California.

To Arthur Edward Waite, author of *The Pictorial Key to the Tarot,* published by Citadel Press, Secaucus, New Jersey.

To Alfred Douglas, author of *The Tarot,* published by Penguin Books of London and New York.

To Manly Palmer Hall, author of *The Secret Teachings of All Ages,* published by The Philosophical Research Society, Los Angeles.

To Gershom Scholem, author of *On the Kabbalah and Its Symbolism,* published by Schocken Books, New York.

To Stuart R. Kaplan, author of *Encyclopedia of the Tarot,* published by U.S. Games Systems, New York.

To Eden Gray, author of *The Tarot Revealed,* published by Signet Books of New York.

To John D. Chambers, translator and editor of *The Divine Pymander and Other Writings of Hermes Trismegistus,* published by Samuel Weiser, New York.

And special thanks to Daniel Bial, Katherine Johnson, and Coral Tysliava at Harper & Row for their fine editorial and production expertise.

To C. G. Leland, author of *Gypsy Sorcery and Fortune-Telling*, published by University Books, New York.

To Barbara Mertz, author of *Red Land, Black Land*, published by Dodd, Mead, New York.

And to Corinne Heline, author of *The Bible and the Tarot*, published by New Age Press, La Cañada, California.

I am also very grateful to the following individuals for their advice, inspiration, or editorial help: Thomas, Julien, and Lauretta Yoseloff, Geraldine Elsa Willigan, Steven Stepak, Edward LeMieux, Darcy Donalan, John Kast, Elizabeth Kast, Sharon Warne, Meg Bessette, Robert Marshall, Susan Reed, Cathy Smith, Susan Clapp, and Michael Dummett.

My thanks also to the Romany cardreaders who told me at least some of their secrets.

Photos of Tarot layouts were provided by Steven P. Stepak of STUDIO 14, Cambridge, Massachusetts.

Forbidden Images

Introduction

Almost all of us have heard of the mysterious Gypsy fortune-telling symbols called Tarot cards. In fact, one way to break the ice at a party is to bring up the subject of Tarot predictions or Tarot symbolism. Soon almost every guest will have a tale to tell or an opinion to express, and of course there will always be a doubting Thomas or two who will try to explain very rationally why such things cannot possibly work to any truly "scientific" person's satisfaction. Meanwhile most of the other guests will find themselves thoroughly fascinated and amazed by an antique Tarot set, if one happens to be available.

For most of us, science only seems to go so far. There is a whole realm of unexplained experience, poetic vision, and intuitive sense that we see and feel around us every day. The idea of psychic power and psychic prediction is no longer the sole pastime of the superstitious; instead, it is a reality that needs to be taken more seriously, a fact of life that should be examined more sensibly. Unfortunately, the mass media have absurdly sensationalized and exploited this delicate subject. They have overloaded us with tall tales and a few famous cases of outright fakes. It is no wonder that many intelligent people have no patience at all with this bizarre and problematic subject.

Reading with Tarot cards does indeed work. Few people with any real experience or knowledge of the subject will deny that. But I don't intend to bore my audience by trying to prove that it does work. Instead, I intend to provide clear, straightforward instruction in the art of Gypsy-style fortune-telling and let people find out for themselves whether it works.

I have found that Tarot readings are much more accurate and powerful than those based on astrology or other forms of occult prediction. But one of the big questions is, How? How do Tarot symbols help us reexamine the past and predict the future? Why do the cards seem to increase psychic powers? What are the secret keys to the Gypsy Tarot cards?

The most important thing to realize about the fortune-telling cards, if one wants to understand the secrets of their power, is that these special icons are not just the outcome of some gambler's pastime invented in the Middle Ages. Instead, they represent the outcome of a much more profound doctrine—a secret and forbidden doctrine—a doctrine that was condemned from almost every pulpit in Christian Europe of the fourteenth and fifteenth centuries.

Just recently, some very convincing symbolic evidence has been uncovered that shows very clearly an ancient origin for the Tarot cards. It seems most probable that Tarot icons were invented or used in Alexandria, a great city in the north of Egypt, well before the time of Christ. It also appears that the Tarot was not originally invented as a fortune-telling tool; instead, it was a masterly designed theological and philosophical teaching device that was based on ancient Egyptian pictorial magic. Later, in the Middle Ages, a device like this would have been called a "philosophical machine" and considered heretical.

But the Europeans had a total misunderstanding of what the cards were really all about; and for that reason the ancient Tarot was soon modified into a game, actually several games, which have survived till this day. For that reason, the forbidden Tarot symbolism has survived with them.

Many occultists have speculated on the power of the Tarot. Tarots were created to be powerful. They are the product of thousands of years of social and cultural experience. And as they say, "An old stone gets very smooth." Tarots work like magic because they are, by their very nature, magical. They are part of primitive "picture magic," or iconography. Later, these magic pictures were raised up and placed in the sky in the form of astrological symbols. Tarot cards also contain astrological symbolism in its perfect ancient order—a whole realm of man's unconscious experience and memory.

Still later, the Egyptians and the Greeks—especially Pythagoras—popularized the idea that numbers are the foundation of all magic and prediction. The Tarot is a tour de force in ancient numerology—probably the most perfect numerological system ever devised. And still later, the Hebrew cabalists claimed that the sacred alphabet contained all the secrets of the universe. In fact, they claimed the universe was created from the sacred alphabetical letters. The Tarot represents that same sacred alphabet; it symbolizes the twenty-two pictures of the ancient Semitic writing. There are twenty-two major Tarot cards and there are twenty-two glyphs in the ancient alphabet.

And still later, the medieval alchemists set as their goal the attainment of the philosophers' stone that enables base metals to be transmuted into gold. We are just realizing that Tarot is a course, perhaps the ultimate course, in the secret symbolism of the alchemical masters.

It was once said that a picture is worth a thousand words. If this is true, imagine for a moment how many words must be contained in twenty-two pictures raised to their factorial! There are just twenty-two cards in the major Tarot, but the number of symbolic ideas contained therein is staggering. Tarot cards predict the future because they attempt to create a symbolic encyclopedia of the entire past. The more one knows about the past, the more one can know about the future. It seems as simple, and as complicated, as that.

1

Some Historical Ideas Regarding Tarot Cards

This book has been designed for those who are beginning with the Tarot—those who are interested in cardreading especially— but those who are more advanced will find it interesting also. It contains the seven great secrets of the symbolism that has been jealously guarded and held by the Gypsies (and a few others) since the destruction of the grand Library at Alexandria in Egypt some sixteen hundred years ago.

THE TRADITIONAL STORY

There is a crucially important traditional story about the Gypsies and the Tarot cards that should be told at the outset, for it sets a pivotal point regarding the history of this magnificent symbolic system.

Sixteen centuries ago in the land of Egypt, there existed a large, powerful, and cosmopolitan city on the north coast called Alexandria. This city was named after the Greek conqueror of Egypt, Alexander the Great. No city in the world could boast of such academic freedom and mixing of the ancient religions and cultures as Alexandria. And no city in the world had a library like that which was built in Alexandria. For in it was a huge storehouse of wisdom and information. And in a special section of the library, in a temple called the Serapeum, was the most precious and powerful of all books: a book that contained the secrets of the sacred alphabet, the secrets of magic, and the secrets of predicting the future with the help of the stars and planets. This book was claimed to have been written by the lord of writing, justice, and magic himself, the ancient Egyptian god Thoth; and for that reason it was called *The Book of Thoth*.

The Book of Thoth contained the essence of all that was magical, mysterious, and forbidden; and it contained the foundation of the ancient pagan religions: the secrets of the true meanings of the Egyptian and Hebrew picture-letters called hieroglyphs. For the history of the universe had been written down by its Creator before the creation itself, and anyone who wished to know of the past or the future must, of course, know the secrets of these pictorial letters used by the ancient priests for writing as well as for magic.

But at the time when our story takes place, the Great Library, the Serapeum, and the precious books within their protective walls were threatened by a powerful new force in the world. Christianity had become the most popular religion in the Eastern Roman Empire; and Egypt was an important part of that great empire.

Christians, in their attempt to create a unique religion, sought to eliminate ideas (and books) they considered offensive or heretical. And, among them, it was well known that the Great Library housed just such pagan thinkers and just such offensive documents.

Those on the other side of this conflict—the Egyptian high priests—soon began to fear for their own safety and for the safety of the ancient scrolls they protected. They were most concerned about the sacred *Book of Thoth*. They knew it was viewed by the constantly growing Christian population as ultimately heretical.

The priests in charge of the library's temple decided that the sacred *Book of Thoth* must be hidden among them in a very secret place—a place far away from the library—in order to save the priceless book from destruction by alien hands. But if the book was hidden, how could it be used? How could it serve its sacred purpose as a teaching device for initiated people?

The high philosophers and priests of Alexandria held an assembly so they might together find a way to solve this problem. At first they thought of confiding the secrets of the system to a group of virtuous people chosen by the high priests. These people, it was hoped, would transmit all of the sacred knowledge from generation to generation until, one day, the ancient wisdom of the Great Library could flourish once again.

But one of the wisest priests stood in the assembly and observed that virtue is a fragile and temporary thing, and difficult to truly find—especially in a continuous family line—so he proposed a more subtle and ingenious idea. He suggested that the sacred symbols (the twenty-two picture-letters that represented all of ancient wisdom) be disguised as a novelty item or as a common toy of children, gamblers, or diviners. For by this method, the magical symbols could be spread to all parts of the known world as quickly as possible.

This priest claimed that children's games, gambling, and attempting to divine the future would never disappear from the earth or fail completely; therefore, why not place the most sacred of all pictorial symbols—*The Book of Thoth* converted into playing-card form—into the hands of the minstrels, jugglers, and children of the world. In this way the sacred symbols of the ancients would survive and be passed from generation to generation even though their owners did not know their true significance or secret meanings. One day in the distant future, the card symbols would be deciphered—understood once again and appreciated for what they really were.

After some thought, this plan was adopted by the council, and it was further suggested that the twenty-two secret symbols (in some versions, seventy-eight) be made and then renumbered in the wrong order to confound all outsiders; then they should be reduced to a smaller size when hand-painted onto the stiff cardlike sheets of heavy papyrus then used for the common games of those times. Many sets of these cards would be made, and in this way they would pass as just another game used by gamblers, children, and diviners—as planned. The work of the initiated artist-priests who made these cards went quickly, and they soon learned that the Council of the Serapeum of Alexandria had only one problem yet to solve: Who would mainly carry the cards, popularize them, and spread them abroad?

Again the wisest priest of the council had a convincing answer. He suggested that the cards be placed in the hands of a people who provided trinkets, games, and entertainment for all the people of the world; in the hands of a people who are free to travel over all the borders of the world; and in the hands of a people who had never been tamed by any foreign culture or material thing.

And in that manner, the ancient Tarot came into the possession of the nearby Alexandrian Gypsies.

Since that time, cardplayers and Tarot readers—good and bad—have transmitted this very secret doctrine from generation to generation far better than a dynasty of the most virtuous people on the earth could have done.

HISTORICAL EVIDENCE

At first sight, this traditional story might seem somewhat far-fetched. But there are bits and pieces of evidence to back it up in just about every respect. We know, for example, that the great Alexandrian library was gravely threatened by Roman and Egyptian Christians some sixteen centuries ago. In fact, the section called the Serapeum was destroyed by order of the Roman emperor Theodosius I in A.D. 389 or 391. The majority of the books in the library were pillaged by the Christians, and there certainly were few left for the Moslems to burn when they ravaged the place some two and a half centuries later. (One version of our traditional story, in fact, blames Moslems, not Christians, for the deadly threat to the library. But the more popular and widespread version, used here, is more in tune with history.)

The destruction of the Great Library stands as one of our worst cultural and intellectual losses. *The Book of Thoth,* and much of the knowledge of the ancient world, was lost to us by the end of the fourth century of our common era.

It is almost certain that Gypsies lived in Alexandria at that time, for they are known to have passed through the land of Egypt. One theory maintains that they were driven out of their original homeland, Northern India, as early as the time of Alexander the Great; and that they had wandered all over the eastern Roman Empire—later, the Byzantine Empire—by the first century of our era. Egypt was part of the eastern Roman Empire for hundreds of years, and it stood in one of the important migration paths of the wandering Gypsy bands.

Gypsies, by the way, most likely got their name *Romany* Gypsies because they were viewed by the Arabs as subjects of Rome ("Roums"—Byzantines); hence, *Romany*. Author Konrad Bercovici—a Gypsy himself—claims that ancient Gypsies applied this name to themselves and have used the words *Rom* (meaning Gypsy man) and *Romany* (the Gypsy language) ever since. The term *Gypsy* is a short version of *Egyptian*, given to the Romany people by the Europeans in the fifteenth century because it was believed Gypsies originated in Egypt.

In ancient times, Gypsies almost certainly had the same basic character that they have today: they were tinkers, horse traders, wanderers, and fortune-tellers. The Persian king Bahram Gor is known to have sold ten thousand captive minstrels, tinkers, and entertainers (most likely, Gypsies) in A.D. 420; and some experts regard this as the earliest known reference to Gypsies.

There is, without a doubt, a definite—and very early—connection between the Gypsies and the Tarot cards. Gypsies first began to enter Western Europe at around the turn of the fifteenth century (1375–1417); and Tarot cards appear there, and begin to be condemned, in just about exactly the same time frame (1377–1423). By the mid-fifteenth century, Tarot cards appear in France, Italy, Switzerland, Germany, and Belgium. It is no coincidence that Tarot cards, and similar cards, appear in almost all countries then populated by the Romany Gypsy bands. For, by that time, the appearance of Gypsies and the appearance of cards seems to go hand in hand.

The earliest accounts of Gypsies in Western Europe describe them as honest—though somewhat tattered—tinkers and fortune-tellers who predict the future by magical means. The earliest accounts of them also say that the first Gypsies in France and elsewhere claimed to be from northern Egypt—the area of Alexandria, in fact.

The Gypsies came into Western Europe at a very unfortunate time: the native population was just recovering from the terrible ravage of a bubonic plague; and fear, superstition, and prejudice were prevalent. Religious intolerance was quite severe, and a time of intense persecution was gestating. Gypsies, although

Christians, had been through every kind of hardship on their trek through the Eastern European countries, but the situation in Western Europe was even more difficult. They were mistaken for black Moors—hated by many Europeans—and they were known to express some pagan-sounding or Gnostic Christian beliefs. Some Gypsies and Jews were accused of stealing children and using them in certain strange magical rites. In this era of savage witch-hunts, such accusations were easily made and widely believed. Xenophobia was rampant; and Gypsies resolutely remained outsiders, by choice and by necessity.

The attitude of the Western Europeans toward the Tarot cards was not much different from their destructive attitude toward the Gypsies: the cards were condemned from just about every church pulpit in the land as some sort of evil influence. Priests dubbed the set of Tarot cards "The Devil's Picture Book" and forbade their use for any purpose in most towns and villages.

Even though the cards were widely condemned in the fourteenth and fifteenth centuries, they became a great favorite with some of the aristocratic families. In fact, two of our oldest surviving sets of Tarot symbols were hand-painted for the royal families of France and, in Italy, Milan. The French pack is called the Gringonneur Tarot, and the Italian deck is called the Visconti-Sforza. These Tarot packs are well over 575 years old, are amazingly accurate in their symbolic layout, and serve as an important reference for those interested in the derivations of early fortune-telling card and playing-card design. Copies of the Visconti-Sforza Pack are still produced today. It is printed in Italy by Grafica Gutenberg expressly for U.S. Games Systems, Inc., of New York, N.Y. 10016.

Another pack, which was probably the set used by the Gypsies and the common people, is called the Tarot of Marseilles. This pack is very accurate in its symbolism, and it is thought to be the ancient prototype from which all of the other good sets of Tarot designed in Europe were copied. These cards are now printed in France by B. P. Grimaud.

And a third set of cards, the Rider-Waite Tarot, is highly recommended, especially to beginners, because it is clear and straightforward in its design, and beautifully rendered from an artistic point of view. Its symbolism was designed in the twentieth century but taken from much older, and accurate, references.

Although Tarot cards were used in Western Europe for at least five centuries, they were so suppressed by the church and the state that very little was known about them by the public at large. The only people who knew a great deal about Tarot cards formed an underground subculture.

The eighteenth century saw the advent of more reasonable laws regarding both the Gypsies and the Tarot pack. There arose a sincere interest in these people, their culture, and the symbolism of their fortune-telling cards. Scholars and mystics began to take an interest in these cards and in the art of understanding their arcane symbolism.

The most important of the eighteenth-century scholars on the Tarot was a French amateur historian named Antoine Court de Gebelin. He wrote a large nine-volume work on the history of the ancients, *Le Monde Primitif,* which was published between the years 1773 and 1784. In the eighth volume of this book he included a section on his study of the Tarot cards. In those pages he said something that was to have an important and lasting effect as far as all further historical research on the Tarot was concerned:

> If one were to know that in our days there existed a work of ancient Egypt, one of their books that escaped malicious destruction . . . a book about their most pure and interesting doctrine, everybody would be eager no doubt to know such an extraordinary and precious work.

This book, he claimed, was the pack of Tarot cards.

Court de Gebelin took notice that several of the major Tarot cards contain ancient Egyptian mythological symbolism. The card called The High Priestess, for example, displays a very dignified female figure with the crown of Isis upon her head. The card called The Wheel of Fortune contains at least three figures that are Egyptian mythological animals.

Although many of Court de Gebelin's theories of the Tarot have been criticized over the years, it seems his is the most satisfactory explanation of the birthplace of these symbols. Other evidence has been discovered since his time which very convincingly backs up his idea of an Egyptian origin. This evidence will be revealed to the reader as we proceed through the meanings of the Tarot major trumps.

Another very important figure who was interested in the secrets of, and the derivations of, the cards, was a defrocked Catholic priest who went by the pen name of Eliphas Levi. In the middle of the nineteenth century, Levi wrote several important books on magic and the occult. Eliphas Levi told us many revealing things about the mysteries of the Gypsy cards. He told us, first of all, that they were very ancient and of an Egyptian-Hebrew-Gnostic derivation. He told us, second, that they were a "book" of ancient and sacred wisdom, connected with magic, numerology, astrology, alchemy, theology, and philosophy. But though he told us all of these things, he supplied us with very little convincing information for proof.

It was also Levi who first pointed out in print that the twenty-two major Tarot cards represent the twenty-two letters of the ancient Semitic alphabet. These letters, the bases of cabalic and numerological mystic systems, were used in the Holy Land as long as four thousand years ago.

Levi published a listing of the twenty-two major Tarot cards that, he claimed, placed them in their correct numerical order. With this order, one was supposed to be able to match the major cards with the symbols of the ancient picture alphabet. The numerical order he published was absurd and obviously wrong. Nevertheless, many people accepted his order. But Levi's major discovery was the *key* to the meaning of the twenty-two major trumps. He discovered the link between the Tarot cards and the *Sepher Yetsirah*.

The *Book of Creation* (or *Sepher Yetsirah*) is a highly symbolic and fascinating sixteen-hundred-word text that describes for us the creation of the universe. Written in Hebrew, the book most likely dates from around the third century. Most experts agree, however, that the spirit of the work derives from a cultural source that is centuries older, because it is strongly influenced by ancient mystical systems from Persia, Mesopotamia, Greece, and Egypt (especially Alexandria).

According to the *Book of Creation*, the twenty-two parts of our universe were created with the magical force of the twenty-two letters of the ancient Hebrew alphabet. The twenty-two parts of the universe were the twelve signs of the zodiac as we know them today, plus the seven planets known to the ancients, plus the primal elements of air, water, and fire. In other words, all of the planets and astrological signs, and three elements (a total of twenty-two), are firmly connected with a corresponding letter of a twenty-two-part picture alphabet.

Each Hebrew letter has a secret and profound symbolic meaning. This is an alphabet whose letters have a spoken (literal) meaning as well as a *symbolic* meaning—much like the Egyptian system of hieroglyphics. Here, letters can be arranged and rearranged in interesting mystical combinations, and this style of arranging Hebrew letters in complex patterns has come to be called "cabalistic."

The *Book of Creation* tells us that before the universe was created, there was the *word,* and that the components of that word are magical alphabetical letters. It also hints that the history of the entire world was *written down before* the actual creation of the world. In this sense, the *Book of Creation* is the key to the past, the present, and the *future.* But, it is claimed, only the highly initiated know how to use it.

Now, what is so interesting about this book's connection with the major Tarot cards is that each related picture-letter has some sort of definite symbol (sign, planet, or element) firmly connected with its already clear symbolism. This, of course, makes each letter a much more powerful and sharply defined symbolic device. If the combined symbolism were weak and vague, it would be difficult to prove that the twenty-two Tarot symbols were connected with it. But, as you will see, many strong, very distinct similarities display themselves as we proceed through the twenty-two major trumps. There are so many vivid symbolic connections here that no one can dismiss them as mere coincidence.

So, while the ancient alphabet is certainly the basic key to the Tarot, the *Book of Creation* is definitely the *master key* to the secrets of the system. And once the master key is located, placing the cards into their correct numerical sequence is no longer that much of a problem.

At this point, one might ask why the numerical sequence is so important. Well, the secrets of the Tarot—all of the most important aspects of this very special system—become greatly clarified once the true sequence of the major cards is known; fortune-teller's meanings, of which some are murky because of great age, gain a clarity and a vividness they have lacked for centuries, at least. And what we get is an intensified Tarot—an old pyramid that has had its peak restored and resharpened.

At this time, no commercial sets of Tarot cards correctly apply the Roman numerals to the major Tarot cards. In most packs, seven or eight of the major trumps have the correct numeration and the remaining trumps are marked incorrectly. The numerical order of today's commercial Tarot packs comes from an old French Tarot set called the Catelin Geofroy Tarot. This order is considered random and untrustworthy because there are other numberings for the Tarot—given before this one was made in 1557—that are very different. This indicates that few people, if anyone, knew the right numeration even as far back as the fifteenth century. If the correct order was known at all, it was known by a limited number of people in the highly initiated circles of a secret society.

But although Tarot packs available today are not correctly numbered, this should not discourage you from buying them and using them. Many are otherwise symbolically accurate, and of course you can change the numbers yourself.

There is one more mystery we have to solve before we can understand the true secret of the symbolism. This secret is the true nature and placement of the most mysterious of all the major Tarot cards: The Fool.

The symbol called "The Fool" is actually the most important card in the Tarot pack. To understand why, we must go back some sixteen hundred years to the threatened Library at Alexandria.

According to traditions about the library, the high priests of the ancient Serapeum were truly worried about the survival of their twenty-two sacred pictorial symbols. So, in order to ensure that the symbolic system would survive, they placed the twenty-two icons, in the form of common playing cards, into the trust of the Gypsies.

Now, the high priests knew that a simple confusion of the numbering of these symbols *alone* would not be enough, for the big problem was that the symbol of the Supreme Being—The Creator of the Universe—was, of course, one of the twenty-two pictures. This was the most important symbol, and no amount of numerical confusion of the icons could hide that fact. The priests had to make a difficult decision: the symbol of the

Supreme Being would have to be disguised, and disguised in such a way that the unenlightened would never recognize what it really represented. Therefore, a picture of a poor, haggard, foolish beggar was substituted in place of the magnificent symbol for The Creator. For what could look more harmless and non-theological than an image of a poor mindless fool? And who would ever suspect that the symbolic system had anything to do with religious beliefs? What reason would there be to destroy and forbid these images when they seemed to propose no definite philosophy?

A famous old Gypsy saying, known even these days, reflects the truth contained in this traditional story:

> The Fool possesses the foolishness of God
> Which is greater than the wisdom of men.

With The Fool and the remainder of the major Tarot so well disguised, the high priests could optimistically hope that all twenty-two images would survive through the dark ages that threatened and be deciphered in a later age when the value of the symbolism could again be understood and accepted.

Over the centuries since that time, the true nature of The Fool card has been kept a strict secret. The correct number for the card also has been kept a secret. Only one author—until now—has even hinted at the true nature and the true number. That was Manly P. Hall, in his *Encyclopedic Outline of Masonic, Hermetic, Qabbalistic, and Rosicrucian Symbolical Philosophy*. And there, he only hinted and speculated. Without this knowledge, one cannot know the most important things about the Tarot cards.

The fifth secret of the Tarot is how the cards are laid out in a symbolic design. I have provided an illustration of this in order to make the general idea clearer.

The card called The Fool is considered to be in a class by itself; therefore, it crowns the entire major Tarot layout. The remaining twenty-one major trumps form seven sets of three cards each called "triads." And these cards are laid out in a linear design beneath The Fool.

Once the cards are laid out in this design—and they are *placed in their correct numerical order*—the mystery of the true Tarot will begin to unveil itself to the interested reader. But the

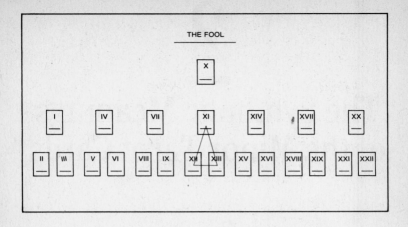

The card called The Fool is really the tenth card of the major Tarot. It crowns the entire set and stands in a class by itself. The twenty-one remaining major trumps are set up as seven sets of triangles in a straight line just beneath the crowning card. Note also that the fourth triad stands at the exact physical center of the symbolic design.

significance of this, and the other two secrets of the Tarot, will be covered later. For now, we must concentrate on the basic things about both the major arcana and the minor arcana, and we must concentrate on the Gypsy art of fortune-telling as it has been practiced over the centuries. Once the basic material is understood, we can better appreciate that which is more advanced in intention.

2

The Symbolic Meanings
of the Minor Tarot Cards

A true Tarot pack is seventy-eight cards. Of these seventy-eight, twenty-two are called "major" Tarot cards (or "major arcana").

The major Tarot cards are easy to identify because they are very striking and colorful pictorial symbols that have titles at the bottom and Roman numerals at the top.

The fifty-six cards that remain in the Tarot pack are called the "minor" Tarot cards. These symbols are very important also, although *minor* might seem to imply otherwise. The minor cards are used extensively in fortune-telling, especially when the diviner wants to know about events that are happening at an everyday or worldly level. The major Tarots, on the other hand, are considered more serious and powerful.

It used to be thought that the twenty-two major Tarot cards are the only part of the pack that has a truly ancient derivation; but lately we have found enough evidence to maintain that the fifty-six minor cards are just as ancient, and that they have always formed a necessary and important part of the Tarot pack.

The minor Tarot is the parent of the common playing cards we use today. The fifty-six minor Tarot cards are divided into four suits similar to the ones we use now: Wands (like our Clubs), Cups (like our Hearts), Swords (like our Spades), and Pentacles (like our Diamonds).

These four suit markings are known to spring from ancient derivations, symbolism that can be traced for over four thousand years through a number of ancient cultures. This means the common poker deck we use today owes much of its symbolism to an extremely ancient, noble, and sacred symbolic discipline that originated in the Holy Land thousands of years ago.

Each of the suits in the minor Tarot is made up of fourteen cards. Four of these fourteen cards are called "picture cards" (but not to be confused with major Tarot cards). These are the King, Queen, Knight, and Page. In a Gypsy fortune-teller's spread, the picture cards in the minor Tarot are usually used to represent people in the person's reading. Most times, one picture card is used to represent the seeker himself. This special picture card is called "the significator."

Each of the four suits in the minor Tarot has a definite and precise symbolic meaning. These symbolic meanings are very important to cardreaders because knowledge of them greatly simplifies remembering the meanings of all fifty-six minor cards. Therefore, each suit marking will now be covered under its own heading.

THE SYMBOLIC MEANINGS OF THE FOUR MINOR TAROT SUITS

THE SUIT OF WANDS

The symbol of the Wand is connected with that which is spiritual, soulful, intuitive, creative, and enterprising. All Wands represent the elements of fire and spirit. In Gypsy Tarot readings, this suit is mostly concerned with the field of human spirit, work, and enterprise.

Like the other three suits, Wands represents one of the four social classes as they were symbolized in ancient and medieval times. The suit of Swords signified the powerful nobility: the rulers, the intellectuals, and the military commanders. The suit of Cups represented the poetic and loving artistic class: the clergy, the teachers, and the highly creative artists or writers. The suit of Pentacles signified the merchants, the townsmen, the burghers, the businessmen in general. The suit of Wands represented the working people, especially the farmers, the peasants, and the servants.

The four picture cards in the suit of Wands represent people with tanned complexions who love the out-of-doors and the country life: farmers, woodsmen, sailors, and healthy, wholesome types in general. These people are almost always in the working class, although they may be unemployed.

Wands represent the season of springtime and the primordial element of fire. On modern cards, Wands is shown as the suit of Clubs.

THE SUIT OF CUPS

The suit of Cups represents the human imagination. The fourteen minor cards with cups on them are connected with our feelings and our emotions. They are primarily the cards of love, romance, poetry, artistic endeavors, instruction, imagination, creation, and regeneration. These are the cards of the artistic, sensitive intellectual class as opposed to the stern legalistic or military ruling classes.

In many Gypsy Tarot readings, the Cups are the traditional symbols of something taking place in the field of art or teaching. At the more down-to-earth level, the Cups are read as being concerned with friendship, romance, harmony, and love.

The four picture cards in the suit of Cups usually represent people who are artistic, poetic, loving, and sensitive. They are usually teachers, clergymen, doctors, musicians, humanitarians, philosophers, poets, artists, or people deeply interested in aesthetics of some kind. Many times, they have a moderate complexion or a ruddy complexion, brown hair, and eyes that run from hazel to blue.

Cups represents the season of summer. They are shown on our modern cards as the suit of Hearts. Cups is the suit of emotion and imagination; therefore, Cups is connected with the magical and primordial element of water.

THE SUIT OF SWORDS

The suit of Swords signifies intellect, decision, judgment, and conflict. At the down-to-earth level, this suit is most concerned with human conflict and trouble in making hard intellectual decisions.

The four picture cards in the suit of Swords represent members of the ruling class—judges, political leaders, military officers, and other people in command.

The Sword is the ancient symbol for intellectual decision, choice, compartmentalization of knowledge, and the resultant conflicts. This suit denotes the ability to make quick, strong, logical, and hardheaded choices—to make value judgments and weigh opposing factors.

This suit describes people who have a city person's complexion—skin that is pale or gray, with dark hair and dark eyes in most cases.

This suit stands for the element air. It also represents the season of winter, and it is displayed on modern playing cards as the suit of Spades.

THE SUIT OF PENTACLES

Pentacles signify that which is physical, practical, and down-to-earth—the physical body and the physical world. The ancient element connected with this suit symbol is earth. Pentacles also signify the season of the harvest: fall. And it is pictured on modern playing cards as the suit of Diamonds. All cards in the suit of Pentacles are connected with things or ideas that are material.

The four picture cards in this suit represent people in the business or mercantile class; these people are usually engaged in profit-making activities like banking, real estate, and finance in general. They are "earthy," sensual, and materially oriented—mainly concerned with sense gratification, sense perception, and worldly security.

People in the suit of Pentacles usually have extreme complexions—quite light or quite dark—and, many times, they have dark eyes and dark hair. Gypsies, however, tend to choose significators on the basis of personality characteristics instead of complexions. Common sense tells us that not all business people have dark hair.

When more than four Pentacle cards fall in a typical Gypsy fortune-teller's spread, this is usually taken as an indication that the seeker will come into a large amount of money.

THE SYMBOLIC MEANINGS OF THE NUMBERS

In ancient times, the symbolism of numbers was crucially important, even to the most ordinary people. The meanings of numbers were taken for granted, just as are the meanings of flags and other insignia today. In fact, the symbolic meanings of numbers, in the old world, were as important to people as the meanings of the constellations in the night sky.

In these early times, numbers were used to represent not only quantities, as in counting and arithmetic, but also important ideas that were considered sacred and profound. Every one of the simple numbers (numbers from one through ten) had its own spirit, poetic meaning, and magical force. Many times this treatment of numbers (like the treatment of Hebrew letters mentioned earlier) is called cabalistic.

THE NUMBER ONE

"One" symbolizes the beginning of all things, the creative power, the center, the First Mover, the Genesis. It was the symbol of creativity and total individuality. It also signified originality, unity, masculine energy and potency, volition, and energy. One was sometimes called "the crown of numbers" because of its determining, ruling, and directive characteristics. The number represented the active, positive male principle—the primary quality— the one from which all others were evolved.

In the minor Tarot pack, all Ones (Aces) represent the beginning, or creation, of something new. They are powerful and energetic cards. The Ace of Swords, for example, signifies the birth or creation of something in the intellectual sphere—the birth of something new in the law, politics, the military, or command.

THE NUMBER TWO

"Two" symbolizes duality, pairing, friendship, sexuality, and receptivity. It is called the dual, female, reflective principle. The number signifies the dualistic world, a place of pairs or opposites: day and night, male and female, positive and negative, good and evil. Many times this duality is explained on the minor cards as a balance of forces or as a meeting of opposite energies. This meeting promises creation, but that creation is not yet fulfilled.

The Two of Cups, for example, betokens a great love affair, a friendship, or a strong emotional meeting.

THE NUMBER THREE

This number was critically important to the ancients because it was the symbol of the triad—the Holy Trinity.

As Lao-Tse declared so long ago, "One engenders two, two engenders three, three engenders all things"; and for this reason the number three has the power to resolve the conflict posed by dualism, to resolve tension, to create synthesis.

"One" represents the father (the creator). "Two" represents the mother (the reflection, the co-creator). And "three" represents the child (the physical world). Therefore, it signifies the fruition, the birth of all things.

Three symbolized growth, unfolding, multiplication, expression, and the fruit produced by way of a partnership or mating. It was represented as a triangle, a symbol of perfection.

Gypsies interpret all pip cards with Threes on them as beneficial and friendly signs. The Three of Cups, for example, is read many times as a token of the fruition of a love affair, a friendship, or an artistic pursuit. It also signifies the coming of a new child.

THE NUMBER FOUR

In most parts of the world, ancient people divided the world into four corners: the four points of the compass. The year was divided into four seasons, and it was thought that the world and everything in it was composed of just four basic elements: earth, air, water, and fire.

The number four also represented the square and the "perfect solid" of the Greek mathematician Pythagoras (the cube). And because of this, four was considered a down-to-earth symbol of measurement, logic, and reason. It was the number of solidarity, reality, order, measurement, classification, and tabulation—"the measuring intelligence."

The Four of Pentacles, for example, is a very strong symbol of material stability and down-to-earth practicality, especially where money or things of material value are concerned. The Four of Swords, on the other hand, denotes powerful abilities of logic and reason, but these are expressed at a down-to-earth and practical level.

THE NUMBER FIVE

This number denotes uncertainty and change, impulsiveness and radicalism, severity and power. Five is the number of uncompleted projects and uncontrolled activity, the symbol of "man after the fall."

Gypsies regard all pip cards with Fives on them as somewhat bad. The Five of Cups, for example, is a severe card, especially where the feelings are involved, because it signifies emotional sorrow and a great deal of uncertainty. The Five of Swords is also a bad card. It denotes an uncontrolled intellect where logic and reason are used for degraded and unjust purposes.

THE NUMBER SIX

This number represents the ideas of harmony, reconciliation, balance, and mediation. It mainly signifies the reconciliation of the two primal opposing forces in nature, and for this reason it has some similarity to the number two. It does not, however, have the intense power of two. The Six of Wands, for example, signifies the harmony of the spirit and the ability to create through the use of diplomacy rather than force.

THE NUMBER SEVEN

This number signifies a temporary rest or cessation after a completed period or cycle, but it is not a symbol of final perfection.

Seven is also associated with power and magical abilities with regard to work and creation. The Seven of Pentacles, for example, is a token of gain and profit through hard work. But the worker knows when to rest, for he is working in harmony with nature instead of against it.

THE NUMBER EIGHT

This number, like the number six, signifies balance; but here more emphasis is placed on the balance of justice and good judgment. Eight is the token of infinite rhythm—alternate cycles of the positive and the negative, involution and evolution. The Eight of Swords, for example, is a card of strife, force, and opposition, as all cards in this suit are; but here the opposition is weakened and balanced out because we realize that the time of opposition is about to end.

The number eight is also known to signify regeneration.

THE NUMBER NINE

This number symbolizes attainment and fulfillment of a goal or a life cycle. It is regarded as being very close to the ultimate perfection, because it is the token of the forces of all the other numbers summed up. The Nine of Wands, for example, is a card symbolizing great preparedness, strength, and stability that cannot be overthrown, especially in matters that have to do with spirit, intuition, and enterprise.

THE NUMBER TEN

This number signifies total purity and perfection, and in this respect it bears some similarity to the number one. Once the number ten is reached, it is understood that we have come round again to unity in the ultimate sense: perfection through completion. We have come to the highest level, the pure and limitless concept.

The Ten card in each suit represents the ultimate expression of that suit. The Ten of Cups, for example, symbolizes the perfection of human love and friendship: great happiness regarding all things on the emotional plane. Pip cards with the number ten are always a welcome sight in a Tarot reading.

3

The Meanings of the Individual Minor Tarot Cards

Over the past several years, a few books have been published which give Tarot meanings that have little to do with Gypsy meanings or traditional interpretations. Many of these lists of meanings represent an obvious attempt to "pretty up" or make more refined that which, in its raw form, is quite plain and almost childlike in its appeal and simplicity. Information on the Tarot that is hundreds of years old is just cast aside in favor of a more polite "psychological approach" or "scientific approach" that really has no basis in reality.

In this book every attempt has been made to get back to the simple, and sometimes crude, old-fashioned Gypsy interpretations. In doing this, however, I have not ignored the work of the great occultists Levi, Christian, Papus, Mathers, or Waite, for their contributions to this knowledge are far too important. No attempt has been made to gloss over some of the more frightening and darker meanings of the symbols, and I have leaned somewhat on some of the older and more reliable documentation on the meanings of these cards.

My choice of minor Tarot illustrations has been dictated by common sense. For the most part, I have chosen the Rider Pack of A. E. Waite. His design, despite some minor problems I have already mentioned, is one of the best now available. The pack is easy to find, and so widely popular that it has certainly proven itself and stood the test of time with the general public all over the western world.

When minor Tarot cards are dealt upside down in a reading, they are usually called "reversed." These reversed cards are usually read as having the opposite meaning of their right-side-up meaning. Sometimes, however, reversed cards are just read as *weaker* than upright cards. The way they are read depends entirely on the intuition of the fortune-teller. There is no hard and fast rule regarding the translation of reversed Tarot cards, so you are welcome to read these reversals in the manner you are most comfortable with.

Each minor Tarot card covered here will be given three symbolic meanings: the primary meaning, the secondary meanings, and the meanings when reversed.

All Kings in the minor Tarot represent men over 25 or 30 years of age. All Queens represent women over 25 or women who have children, regardless of their age. All Knights represent people of either sex who are young adults. And all Pages represent children of either gender, and they are usually under 13 years of age.

ACE OF WANDS

Primary Meaning. The Ace of Wands signifies the birth of the spirit, of intuitive energy, the creative power of the human spirit. Originality, individuality, potency, and volition regarding things connected with spirit, intuition, and enterprise. Gypsies also regard this as a card that betokens agricultural fertility. A strong, positive, happy card.

Secondary Meanings. The beginning of an enterprise, creation, or invention. The power of fire. Innovation, initiative, revelation, glory, feasting, energy, and growth. Many times the card signifies the coming of a new career.

Reversed Meanings. The card is weaker, or opposite, of those meanings given above: clouded joy, false starts, that the enterprise will fail, the spirit lies sleeping.

TWO OF WANDS

Primary Meaning. The Two of Wands symbolizes a friendship, a love, a partnership—all related to spiritual awareness, intuition, or enterprise. There may be opposition from this friend or partner. But remember, "Opposition is true friendship."

Secondary Meanings. The spiritual versus the material worlds. The idealist must cope with the real world. Spirit and energy in its most exalted form. Good fortune, riches, opulence.

Reversed Meanings. The subject of the reading (called "the seeker") may be dominated by a friend. A good friendship, or a partnership, may not bear fruit. Caution against impatience is advised. Otherwise, a reversal of this card can signify meanings weaker than those listed as primary.

THREE OF WANDS

Primary Meaning. The Three of Wands is a symbol of work and cooperation with a friend that has borne fruit. It signifies the realization of a spiritual or mystical adventure through cooperation with another.

Secondary Meanings. Cooperation in business or an enterprise has brought established strength and the end of troubles. A sign that collaboration will favor enterprise. Trade and commerce will flourish. There will be new growth. There will be a very good harvest. All cooperative efforts in the field of agriculture will yield great results. The basis of the work is now firmly established and the undertaking can be continued without fear.

Reversed Meanings. Weaker or opposite of that above: Beware of help offered, there may be unfair dealing and disappointment, failure of nerve, paralysis of will.

FOUR OF WANDS

Primary Meaning. The Four of Wands signifies a solid and down-to-earth kind of spiritual life, intuitive talent, or enterprising nature. This is best described as a simple country life where one works in harmony with and appreciation of nature, as in the field of agriculture.

Secondary Meanings. The bounty of the harvest home. The haven of refuge. Domestic tranquility, security, happiness, peace, and prosperity. Logical, rational, and perfected work all in harmony with nature. Good society, union, association, family spirit.

Reversed Meanings. Weaker or opposite of those above: obstacles, discord, lack of common sense, disharmony with nature.

FIVE OF WANDS

Primary Meaning. The Five of Wands symbolizes competition, adversity, uncertainty, and change, especially in the fields of agriculture, business, or enterprise. Not a good card for country lovers, farmers, or naturalists, it denotes shiftlessness, inconsistency, lack of control, and change for the worse.

Secondary Meanings. The battle of life. Quarrel with a neighbor. Wild competition. Tough legal proceedings. Trickery, contradiction, dispute, severity, but victory if one can surmount all of this.

Reversed Meanings. Advise the seeker to beware of trickery and cheating, for this reversal denotes fraud, litigation, contradiction, and defeat of an enterprise by way of underhanded tactics. When the card is found reversed in an otherwise happy reading, Gypsies read it as "a love of games and exercise."

SIX OF WANDS

Primary Meaning. Victory after strife. Great success in undertakings of the spirit, intuitive creation, or enterprise through the use of diplomacy rather than force. A symbol of peacemaking activities by a spiritual, intuitive, and innovative leader.

Secondary Meanings. Understanding combined with love and intuition will produce great results. Harmony of the spirit. Old friends will be reconciled. Good news. A triumphal procession. New advancements in enterprise and agriculture after hard times. There will be increasing harmony in relationships. Hopes will be fulfilled. Expectations will be crowned.

Reversed Meanings. Apprehension and fear, especially in the areas of enterprise, farming, and trade. Great concern about treachery within one's own company. Apprehension regarding the hidden activities of "the competition" and foes in business. Bad news and great delay regarding all things covered above.

SEVEN OF WANDS

Primary Meaning. The Seven of Wands signifies a strong, solid resting place that has been attained after a period of hard work. A token of the stalwart spirit, intuitive and mystical, that cannot be overthrown.

Secondary Meanings. Great power, strength, and courage. One will hold his own against adversaries by means of faith and valor. There will be opposition, but the seeker will emerge victorious by virtue of his special gifts of wisdom and fortitude. Sometimes he must stand totally alone while severely opposed. There may be verbal strife, a war of trade, and negotiations.

Reversed Meanings. Beware of perplexity and indecision. Timidity will cause defeat. Hesitation will result in the loss of an opportunity. Anxiety, embarrassment, confusion, all connected with spirit, agriculture, or enterprise.

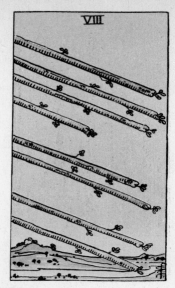

EIGHT OF WANDS

Primary Meaning. The Eight of Wands signifies a swift, just, and balanced spiritual makeup. It denotes quick and graceful activity in all undertakings related to the suit of Wands. Fast decisions will be made with fine judgment, understanding, fairness, and sure direction.

Secondary Meanings. Speed toward an end that promises rewards. Haste, quick communication, sophisticated mental activity. Understanding, observation, direction. Activity in undertakings. That which is on the move. Some say this Wand is the "arrows of love," but that depends on the nature of the surrounding cards.

Reversed Meanings. Weaker or opposite of those above. Arrows of jealousy. Domestic quarrels. Break of a friendship. Injustice. Guilt.

NINE OF WANDS

Primary Meaning. The Nine of Wands symbolizes an almost complete attainment and fulfillment of a goal or of a complete life cycle. It signifies great preparedness, security, and stability which cannot be overthrown. All of this is connected with the realm of spirit, intuition, the country life, and enterprise. Opposition will be put down because the seeker is an established and formidable opponent.

Secondary Meanings. Good health. Strength in reserve. Order. Discipline. Good arrangement. Continued success. High energy. All related to the suit of Wands.

Reversed Meanings. The seeker is not well prepared. Delay, obstacles, adversity, weakness, obstinacy, calamity, a lack of adaptability. Otherwise the meanings are weaker than the upright meanings.

TEN OF WANDS

Primary Meaning. Here, Waite's design shows a secondary meaning. The Ten of Wands is actually the symbol of the total perfection of the spiritual individual. It is a very happy card for those with the Wands nature: spirited, enterprising lovers of nature. More emphasis needs to be placed on the positive aspects of this card.

Secondary Meanings. Aspirations toward perfection have become a burden. The weight of this load is too heavy for most people to carry; therefore, this card has become the token of the burden unwisely chosen. The seeker has taken too much upon himself. He is not psychologically suited to his work. He is heavy with worry and fear. He will, however, reach his goal.

Reversed Meanings. A clever person who shifts burdens from himself to others. One who exploits and oppresses. Lies, propaganda, deceit—all designed to disrupt the ordered affairs of others. A traitor, a disguise, a liar.

PAGE of WANDS.

PAGE OF WANDS

Primary Meaning. The Page of Wands represents a spirited, nature-loving, intuitive child who is both enterprising and honest. Many times he has a tanned, healthy, country person's complexion.

Secondary Meanings. The child is creative, and loves to tell stories, bring good news, or bring friendly gossip. This Page will sometimes act as an envoy, is very enthusiastic, and has a spirited, dynamic personality. The child will be helpful to the seeker.

Reversed Meanings. A child who can't keep a secret, and one who may betray a trust. One with a love for mean gossip and scandal. A superficial and unstable child. Bad news.

KNIGHT of WANDS.

KNIGHT OF WANDS

Primary Meaning. The Knight of Wands represents a young person of either sex who is no longer a child—attractive, strong, healthy, and usually tanned. This Knight is very intuitive, spiritual, country-loving, and enterprising.

Secondary Meanings. This Knight is a defender of the spiritual side of life and may cause some changes: a change of residence, of outlook, or of location. He or she is basically friendly and loves to initiate things. He can sometimes be a bit hasty and impetuous—even fiery—but makes a generous friend or lover.

Reversed Meanings. A young person, not attractive, who is far too hasty and impetuous. This reversal implies quarreling, breakup, or refusal to give another his or her freedom. The Knight is described as jealous, mean, unfriendly, unsupportive, and narrow-minded. Opposite of the Knight when right side up.

QUEEN of WANDS.

QUEEN OF WANDS

Primary Meaning. The Queen of Wands symbolizes a spiritually oriented, highly intuitive, and enterprising woman who is a lover of the outdoor life and the world of nature in general. She has a healthy, tanned complexion and is described as honest, attractive, chaste, home-loving, spirited, friendly, and magnetic.

Secondary Meanings. If the card beside her is a man, she is very fond of him; if it is a woman or a child, she is somehow interested in their welfare. Many times, people from the suit of Wands are from working-class or agricultural backgrounds. When found "well placed" in a reading, they are described as honest, attractive, friendly, and virtuous.

Reversed Meanings. She is too economical and strict. Many times she is described as vain, unfaithful, overbearing, domineering, sarcastic, and sharp. However, when reversed she can be read as a weaker version of the upright meanings.

KING of WANDS

KING OF WANDS

Primary Meaning. The King of Wands signifies a good man—often a country gentleman—who is primarily spiritual and intuitive. He is a leader in fields connected with natural science or related enterprise. He is healthy, agile, passionate, attractive, ethical, and energetic. Many times, he is a fiery, high-spirited man.

Secondary Meanings. This King can give good advice and counsel. He is austere but tolerant, strict but fair, ascetic but good-humored. When upright, he is always described as extremely honest and a good father. Many times, members of the suit of Wands are animal lovers.

Reversed Meanings. When reversed, the Gypsies compare him with Julius Caesar, but the adjectives used may not be fair to Caesar: cold, prejudiced, narrow, autocratic, tyrannical, ruthless, severe, and hot-tempered.

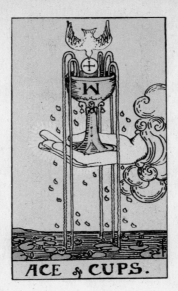

ACE ⚜ CUPS.

ACE OF CUPS

Primary Meaning. The Ace of Cups signifies the beginning of great emotional happiness, the birth of a love relationship; the coming of joy, contentment, pleasure, and good cheer. It symbolizes the birth of the poetic and the artistic, the feelings and the emotions, the imaginative, and all things of the heart.

Secondary Meanings. Fertility, productiveness, beauty, love, protection, passion, inspiration, abundance, feasting, nourishment, all in their beginning stages. It, like the card called The Empress, can signify the conception of a child.

Reversed Meanings. A reversal is usually read as weaker than that above; otherwise, the meanings are very sad: unrequited love, sterility, false heart, instability, revolution, an overturning of the present state.

TWO OF CUPS

Primary Meaning. The Two of Cups signifies a very strong emotional pairing—usually a serious love relationship. It may also symbolize a partnership in the arts, a friendship, or an emotional bond to another person.

Secondary Meanings. The harmony of the male and female in the ideal sense. Balanced emotions. Emotional affinity, receptivity, empathy, and trust. Reflection, harmony, marriage, ecstasy, affection, attachment, lovemaking, union, sympathy, and reciprocity.

Reversed Meanings. A betrayal of trust. Separation, divorce, unfaithfulness, deceit, bad communication, misunderstanding, jealousy, revenge, violent passion. The reversal can also be read as weaker than the meanings when upright. It's not a good idea to read "bad reversals" until one has a good deal of experience.

THREE OF CUPS

Primary Meaning. The Three of Cups signifies the coming into being of something that was conceived in love, artistic effort, or deep emotion: a child, a work of art, a lasting friendship. The fruition of a love relationship.

Secondary Meanings. Fulfillment, realization of love, that love is mutual, great happiness resulting from an emotional pairing, healing power, the conclusion of a matter of the feelings in plenty. A token of good luck in love.

Reversed Meanings. Excess of physical enjoyments, unbridled passion, lack of temperance, selfish exploitation of the affection of others, sensuality without love. Weaker or opposite of the upright meanings.

FOUR OF CUPS

Primary Meaning. The Four of Cups denotes that emotions have been subordinated by logic and that reason prevails over feelings. Not a happy card where feelings, love, and emotion are involved. Love is turning to familiarity.

Secondary Meanings. The "magic" has gone from a love relationship. Fulfillment has reached its peak and can go no further. Boredom with a lover. Discontent with artistic or sensual pleasures. Displeasure, aversion, imaginary vexations. One who thinks too much and loves too little.

Reversed Meanings. Novelty, new relations, new love, excesses of all kinds. Lack of discernment and taste. Overindulgence.

FIVE OF CUPS

Primary Meaning. The Five of Cups is a severe card where emotions are involved. It denotes uncertainty and lack of control in one's romantic, artistic, or emotional life. It also signifies sorrow or loneliness. A card of loss but with something remaining.

Secondary Meanings. Broken engagement, bad marriage, voluntary loneliness, rejection of pleasure, unkindness from friends, emotional uncertainty, loss of a loved one. Traditionalists say alternatives remain; there is a need for the reassessment of one's life, followed by a major change.

Reversed Meanings. The cups of happiness are overturned. Gypsies compare this reversal with the tragedy of Romeo and Juliet: despair, ill luck, vain regret, bitterness, frustration.

SIX OF CUPS

Primary Meaning. The Six of Cups denotes a healthy emotional balance and harmony that is mainly due to happy experiences in childhood or happy recollections from the past. This idea of harmony, balance, and reconciliation also applies to things connected with love and the arts.

Secondary Meanings. A card of nostalgia and reminiscence where things of the past bring pleasure to the relationships of the present. Gypsies often say this card denotes a happy meeting with a dear childhood friend. Pleasure, harmony of natural forces without effort or strain, equilibrium, happy couple, pleasant memories.

Reversed Meanings. Emotional or artistic failure because of an inability to adapt to changing conditions. Clinging to the past. Outworn morals and manners. The desire for that which is gone and can never return. Emotions out of balance. Inability of lovers to reconcile.

SEVEN OF CUPS

Primary Meaning. The Seven of Cups signifies a very powerful, dramatic, poetic, and artistic imagination combined with a strong, solid emotional makeup. It indicates remarkable vision and almost magical abilities in the areas of love, emotional sensitivity, and creative abilities in the arts.

Secondary Meanings. There is a hunger for that which is beautiful, and one feels at home and at rest when surrounded by beauty. The seeker may be psychic or clairvoyant. Visions, fantasy, imagination, reflection, ideas, meditation.

Reversed Meanings. Self-deception in matters of love, the emotions, or the arts. Reliance on false hopes. Daydreaming and foolishness. Self-delusion. Hyperimagination. Illusion.

EIGHT OF CUPS

Primary Meaning. The Eight of Cups symbolizes emotional calmness, balance, and peace of mind because one lives in accord with his or her emotional cycles. A card of modesty, mildness, detachment, gentleness, joy, and pleasure.

Secondary Meanings. A turning away from established, conventional relationships in order to progress to something newer and deeper. The rejection of links with the past which have outlived their relevance. Rejection of material success. Fairness, justice, and equality in love.

Reversed Meanings. Great feasting, worldliness, pleasure-seeking, partying, and flirting. One who chases around after vague, impossible ideals, especially in the areas of love, sexual attraction, or the arts. Restlessness and dissatisfaction which leads to the abandonment of a love which is well founded.

NINE OF CUPS

Primary Meaning. The Nine of Cups signifies the attainment and fulfillment of a romantic, artistic, or emotional goal. The seeker's emotional well-being is almost perfect; almost all problems and difficulties have been surmounted. Contentment, stability, liberality, and security.

Secondary Meanings. A love of sensual pleasure. A promise of good health. Goodwill. Happiness in general. Wishes fulfilled. Physical well-being.

Reversed Meanings. Overindulgence, vanity, complacency, self-satisfaction, extreme sentimentality. One who overlooks the faults of others and is easily taken advantage of. Sometimes Gypsies say this reversal means danger of a robbery.

TEN OF CUPS

Primary Meaning. The Ten of Cups symbolizes the perfection of human love, emotional well-being, and artistic creativity. All this has been well earned. A happy, loving family life; peace; security; trust.

Secondary Meanings. Purity of the heart, individuality, honor, esteem, virtue, glory, good reputation, well-earned security. Another token of very good fortune.

Reversed Meanings. Strife, opposition, anti-social actions, disruption, manipulation, exploitation, criminal actions, indignation, rage, combat, sorrow, "house of the false heart."

PAGE of CUPS.

PAGE OF CUPS

Primary Meaning. The Page of Cups denotes a poetic, imaginative, and artistic boy or girl who is primarily emotional, gentle, and kind. Here, the Page holds a chalice from which a fish appears; this icon signifies the imagination. Many times, people in the suit of Cups have medium complexions and brown hair. Eye color usually runs from hazel to blue.

Secondary Meanings. A poetic youth with a talent for art or music; studious, thoughtful, romantic, gracious, and sensitive. This Page could bring good news or render service to the seeker. Many times described as a "fair child."

Reversed Meanings. The child is now a rebellious youth who has good taste but no discipline, a tease who hurts those who love him, a lover of luxury. The child flits from one thing to the other but never settles on anything.

KNIGHT of CUPS.

KNIGHT OF CUPS

Primary Meaning. The Knight of Cups has been described as the Sir Lancelot of the Tarot. The card describes a young adult who is a champion of the artistic, the poetic, and the romantic. This person is friendly, attractive, and open to new ideas. Sometimes a lover from a faraway place.

Secondary Meanings. A romantic skilled in the arts. A bringer of ideas. This Knight may bear a message or make an advance, a proposition, or an invitation. Love may come from him (or her) to the seeker. An attractive individual with high principles.

Reversed Meanings. A young romantic far too easily led. This person is not so attractive because he shows the inability to know where truth ends and falsehood begins. An artificial person—swindling, tricky, fraudulent, and seductive. More like a Don Giovanni than a Sir Lancelot.

QUEEN OF CUPS

Primary Meaning. The Queen of Cups denotes a very loving and sensitive woman who is primarily emotional. She loves poetry, art, and things of the imagination. She dreams, but she acts on her dreams.

Secondary Meanings. A gentle, good-natured woman who may be interested in—or render service to—the seeker. She is described as a good wife, a loving mother, a favorite teacher. She is kind and full of feeling. A striking and beautiful "fair" woman who has the gifts of vision, loving intelligence, and emotional wisdom.

Reversed Meanings. Here, she is far too easily influenced. She has no common sense. She is too much of a dreamer: ethereal, absentminded, and out of touch. Waite goes so far as to accuse her of dishonor, vice, perversity, and depravity, with artistic and poetic talent gone to waste.

KING of CUPS.

KING OF CUPS

Primary Meaning. The King of Cups signifies a sensitive and artistically creative man. He is an emotional individual, but also philosophical and idealistic. He is noted for his kindness, liberality, and generosity. And he is the kind of man who invites respect.

Secondary Meanings. An attractive, loving man. He may be interested in the seeker. Many times, he likes to work behind the scenes alone, but he is skilled in the ways of the world. Often he is a teacher or an artist, sometimes a skilled craftsman. "A good, fair man."

Reversed Meanings. This King has a violent artistic temperament. He is egotistical and a rogue, dishonest, insensitive, boorish, and cruel. Infidelity and scandal also enter the picture.

ACE OF SWORDS

Primary Meaning. The Ace of Swords signifies the birth of intellectual judgment and reasoning power. It denotes the creation of, or the beginning of, rational ability, justice, authority, decision-making, and intellectual conflict. It is always a symbol of strong rational force.

Secondary Meanings. The beginning of any mental or logical procedure, but many times there is a strong element of conflict connected with this suit. The forcing of change. The making of hard decisions. The struggle of rational over irrational forces. The start of argument and adversity. Intellectual victory.

Reversed Meanings. All the negative aspects of wanton power: injustice, stupidity, overthrow of just authority, restriction imposed by force or fear, brute force, violence, destruction. But the reversal can just be read as weaker than the upright meanings.

TWO OF SWORDS

Primary Meaning. The Two of Swords represents a harmonious mating of intellectual forces: a rational balance. The interplay of powerful opposing forces. The friendship of two brilliant, authoritative, and intellectually creative people.

Secondary Meanings. Peace restored. Stalemate, truce, indecision, equilibrium, victory without conflict. Tenderness and affection by way of intense strength and balance. Harmony of powerful and commanding forces.

Reversed Meanings. The deliberate stirring up of trouble. Love of discord and tension for its own sake. Lack of intellectual self-control. Release in movement, but there is an aura of impending danger. Trickery, falsehood, imposture, disloyalty. An argument causes a break with a friend.

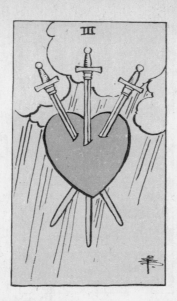

THREE OF SWORDS

Primary Meaning. The Three of Swords signifies that the intellectual pairing of logic and reason has yielded real results at the substantial level: inventions, ideas, theories, solutions, math, science, books, maps, and so on. Logic and reason, however, can be tough on the emotions, hence Waite's sad picture of a pierced heart.

Secondary Meanings. Intellectual birth through discord and strife. Growth through mental conflict and trouble. Rational strength and courage have yielded results, but stormy weather may be ahead for the emotions and affections.

Reversed Meanings. Error, distraction, misunderstanding, language barrier, confusion, lack of communication, disorder, alienation, discord, strife, and war—all for stupid reasons.

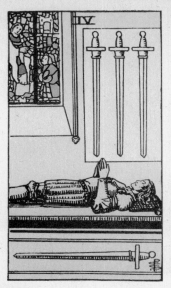

FOUR OF SWORDS

Primary Meaning. The Four of Swords signifies a solid and down-to-earth attitude regarding the hard intellectual struggle we have been describing: a more practical, comfortable, and restful viewpoint. The figure pictured here is shown in a state of peace and repose. This is a very powerful card, denoting logical and mental capabilities of a high order.

Secondary Meanings. Peace and order established through law and justice. Firm administration in troubled times. Retreat from mental strife. Very practical and realistic intelligence. Quiet solitude.

Reversed Meanings. The struggle will begin again. Renewed activity. The beginning of a new plan. But there will be precaution, economy, and care.

FIVE OF SWORDS

Primary Meaning. The Five of Swords denotes complete loss of rational and intellectual control, with defeat after a fierce struggle. It is a severe and bad card—perhaps the worst in the whole Tarot.

Secondary Meanings. Logic and reason are used for degraded and unjust purposes. Severity is met with severity. Sadness, affliction, and defeat are the results. Loss, failure, slander, treachery, malice, bitterness, sorrow.

When the card is well placed (surrounded by good cards), its meaning is not so somber and severe.

Reversed Meanings. Opposite or weaker than those above. If the card is badly placed, however, the meanings are even worse: crisis, disaster, destruction, bereavement, degradation, mourning.

SIX OF SWORDS

Primary Meaning. The Six of Swords denotes harmony and balance on the mental plane. Understanding, gentleness, and reconciliation have won the battle against severity and power. There is an escape from sorrow, a passage away from difficulties, a libation (perhaps only temporary) from mental conflict.

Secondary Meanings. Travel away from trouble, perhaps travel over the water. Escape from sorrow. Temporary liberation. The future will be better. Immediate problems have been solved; some major obstacles overcome. A proposal of love. Peace after a bitter conflict. Envoy of peace. Journey for peace.

Reversed Meanings. There is a need for continued struggle, effort, and fortitude. Attempts to escape from difficulties will not succeed. There is no way out of present difficulties. Troubles may become public. There may be an unwanted legal or romantic proposal. There may be a need for a confession or a declaration.

SEVEN OF SWORDS

Primary Meaning. The Seven of Swords symbolizes a triumph of the inspired intellect. A cycle of mental activity is completed and perfected. Craft and cleverness have overcome darker forces. Divine inspiration. There is a rest from conflict and force. There is also maturity and a control of power.

Secondary Meanings. Victory by means of an ingenious plan. Destruction of evil by very subtle methods. A trick has been played on the unjust. The triumph of cunning. Magical aspirations.

Reversed Meanings. Loss of nerve. A reluctance to follow through on a daring course of action when it is most needed. Failure of a plan. Unstable effort. Foolish attempt at theft. Unwise counsel. Hesitancy, cowardice, and surrender immediately before a victory would have been won.

EIGHT OF SWORDS

Primary Meaning. The Eight of Swords denotes a deep intellectual balance. Here, one can see the alternate cycles of the positive and the negative regarding almost any question or conflict. Sometimes, however, this balanced and philosophical outlook causes problems in making decisions.

Secondary Meanings. The seeker alternates between one opinion and another that opposes. Shortened mental force. Rational restriction. Inability to make a decision. Something is holding the seeker down, but this can be patiently overcome. Changes for the better are coming into one's life, but opportunities must be grasped. A good card, denoting a deep sense of justice.

Reversed Meanings. Unfairness. Severe intellectual criticism. Opposition. Unforeseen perils. Fear of censure. Fatalism. A state of mental depression.

NINE OF SWORDS

Primary Meaning. The Nine of Swords symbolizes something far less severe than that pictured. It signifies complete and near-perfect rational and logical strength arising from stress, conflict, doubt, and powerful assertion.

Cards that are strong on pure intellectualism are usually given rather awful meanings by the traditionalists, but more emphasis needs to be put on their positive side. Experienced Gypsy readers usually stress optimism.

Secondary Meanings. Problems, despair, suffering. The struggle of all living things; it brings new strength and new life out of suffering. At its worst, this is a card of utter desolation, complete isolation from help and comfort, miscarriage, and death. It is never read this way by Gypsy fortune-tellers, but just stands as a somewhat morbid reminder of mortality. It seems the main message Gypsy readers want to convey is that intense mental insight can bring suffering. The Gypsies are very suspicious of logic alone.

Reversed Meanings. Weaker than those above.

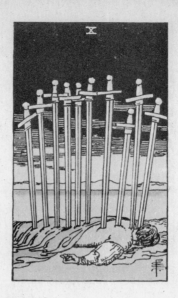

TEN OF SWORDS

Primary Meaning. The Ten of Swords is the symbol of total intellectual perfection and logical infallibility—hard rationality at its purest and highest level.

Secondary Meanings. Gypsy readers sometimes take a very dim view of this card, and Waite's version of the symbol certainly looks uninviting. When well placed, however, this is a very good card that denotes mental brilliance and pure logic. On the other hand, a Gypsy reader would certainly point out that we live in a very scientific and logic-oriented world—a world of the "infallible computer"—and yet we sit near the edge of total catastrophe. Meanings are: misfortune, disruption, ruin, pain, and death. But this generally refers to a group or community instead of to an individual.

Reversed Meanings. Recovery, better health, insight, power, authority, revolution, overthrow of evil, hard decisions, survival plans. But good things are temporary unless law and justice are preserved.

PAGE OF SWORDS

Primary Meaning. The Page of Swords represents a child who has outstanding intelligence and capability of judgment. The child is usually described as one who has diplomacy and understanding beyond his years.

Secondary Meanings. A child of either sex who is brilliant, skilled, keen-sighted, and fair. The child is also described as attractive, graceful, slender, and sometimes introverted. This young person is very protective of the seeker and sometimes acts on the seeker's behalf, even to the extent of keeping a watchful eye on others. Many times, they have a pale complexion and brown hair, but the physical characteristics are not so important as the personality description.

Reversed Meanings. A nervous, high-strung child with a tendency to frivolity and cunning. This young person may not be in good health (or may not appear healthy) and may turn out to be an imposter or spy. A deceitful, competitive, unpredictable, but crafty child.

KNIGHT of SWORDS .

KNIGHT OF SWORDS

Primary Meaning. The Knight of Swords describes a young person who is brilliant and perceptive—one who cannot be deceived. He or she is a bold, strong, dominant person who rushes headlong into the seeker's life. This knight is always a champion in times of conflict and strife. A commanding personality with outstanding qualities of logic and intellect.

Secondary Meanings. This Knight is dramatic, dedicated to the ones he loves, and he may come to the defense of the seeker with great skill, capacity, courage, and decisive ability. He is a winner, and no obstacles will stand in his way. Many times he is in a position of authority and command. The Knight of Swords, like all other picture cards in this suit, is usually a slim, agile, active person with a light or pale complexion.

Reversed Meanings. A young adult who is pushy, impulsive, extravagant, and domineering. A braggart who has little to brag about. A bully who is quick to get into trouble. A tyrant who is fierce in action and intention but has no permanent power.

QUEEN of SWORDS.

QUEEN OF SWORDS

Primary Meaning. The Queen of Swords signifies an attractive, intellectual woman who is said to be "wise beyond her years." Her countenance is severe but beautiful. She is perceptive, bright, and confident; she loves detail and accuracy and has a talent for law, politics, or command.

Secondary Meanings. She can be strict with those around her, but also gentle and fair. It is said by some that she is familiar with sorrow and can possibly be a widow. She has a strong sense of justice and takes a logical and rational view of things. She is not the kind of woman that is easily fooled or taken advantage of. Her maturity and wisdom have earned her a good deal of respect.

Reversed Meanings. A woman who is brilliant but bitter and revengeful; this can make her a formidable enemy. She is described as hard, cold, deceitful, and slanderous; and at other times as a dour, sad woman of authority who is a prude.

KING of SWORDS.

KING OF SWORDS

Primary Meaning. The King of Swords represents a man of high mental capabilities. He is strict, perceptive, logical, fair, and he is usually connected with authority, command, the law, or the military. He is usually over 25 years of age, and is often a father figure.

Secondary Meanings. This King is inventive, original, rational, and sometimes radical. There is a suggestion of supremacy and force, but he is fair and merciful. This man could be a lawyer, judge, teacher, political leader, military officer, or some other kind of commander. He is an attractive man with a light, or pale, city person's complexion, and he is usually in very good physical condition. He is an assertive, dynamic man and may befriend the seeker.

Reversed Meanings. An overbearing and unjust man who will produce chaos in the name of order. He is capable of conflict, violence, cruelty, and overthrow. His brilliant mind makes him one to beware of, for his negative ways can be very subtle.

ACE OF PENTACLES

Primary Meaning. The Ace of Pentacles denotes the beginning of, or the creation of, material prosperity. It signifies the birth of physical security, wealth, material comfort, and contentment.

Secondary Meanings. The card is a token of new wealth, an inheritance, a profitable business venture, appreciation of physical beauty, sensuousness, the ability to create in solid, down-to-earth senses, and the birth of physical endurance. Pentacles are usually regarded as tokens of money, but their true meaning is wider.

Reversed Meanings. A lack of faith in anything beyond this world. Gross materialism. Also miserliness, avarice, greed, extremely fixed patterns of thinking and behavior. This reversal, like all others, can be read as weaker than the upright meanings.

TWO OF PENTACLES

Primary Meaning. The Two of Pentacles symbolizes cooperation, grace, and adaptability regarding matters of material security.
It can represent pairing and friendship connected with matters
of physical prosperity.

Secondary Meanings. Social grace in handling situations related
to money or security. A partnership or friendship regarding a
business. Skill in the art of finance: adaptability, dexterity,
harmony. The ability to deal with change in a balanced and
lighthearted manner. The ability to work with others in matters
of material prosperity: investments, contracts, negotiations, and
business in general. Making friends and influencing people.

Reversed Meanings. Clumsy handling of business matters.
Failure to communicate well. Enforced gaiety, simulated enjoyment, inconsistency, lack of consideration for another, reckless-
ness, overindulgence, lack of receptiveness.

THREE OF PENTACLES

Primary Meaning. The Three of Pentacles represents the fruit of one's labors at the physical level—the growth, the unfolding, the expression of human ideas at the material level. It is the card of craftsmen, architects, engineers, and of all people who create physical things or bring abstract ideas into material reality.

Secondary Meanings. Excellence, renown, and recognition as a craftsman. Wealth, nobility, aristocracy obtained through skill as a craftsman. One who will gain great security because of his craft. Gratitude, fame, celebration because of high material skill—and this can count for the arts also.

Reversed Meanings. Poor workmanship. Mediocrity in one's craft. Laziness, shallowness, and conceit connected with work. A job that is a failure through one's own fault. Financial troubles because of this.

FOUR OF PENTACLES

Primary Meaning. The Four of Pentacles is a very strong symbol of complete material stability, prosperity, and power. It betokens a totally solid and down-to-earth kind of security. It signifies a very high aptitude for business and things connected with the physical plane.

Secondary Meanings. The surety of possessions. Money will be gained through the use of common sense. A commercial or financial establishment will flourish. The seeker will do well in business. Established money. Staying with that which one already has. Money problems will be overcome.

Reversed Meanings. Delay, suspense, obstacles, and opposition regarding possessions or money. Extreme love of money or material things, miserliness, fear of loss, covetousness, over-centralization of power.

FIVE OF PENTACLES

Primary Meaning. The Five of Pentacles symbolizes uncertainty and loss of control regarding money and other material things. It is a bad card, denoting material trouble, poverty, and destitution. And again, much of this is beyond the seeker's control.

Secondary Meanings. Loss of security. Inability to find work. But new friendships may be formed with those in similar circumstances. Some say that lovers may be brought together by similar material problems. The problems of poverty are severe, but this card denotes they can be escaped.

Reversed Meanings. Discord, disorder, squalor, chaos. Lovers will not be able to marry. Marital problems because of infidelity, or as an old-style Gypsy might put it: "A mistress may call upon her lover's wife and threaten the marriage." All these troubles are said to be caused by dullness and obstinacy.

SIX OF PENTACLES

Primary Meaning. The Six of Pentacles represents a harmony and a balance when dealing with things of the material world. It signifies the gratitude of the wise when they have been well favored by fortune. And this gratitude expresses itself as sympathy, kindness, charity, and equity.

Secondary Meanings. Balance and mediation in material affairs. Philanthropy, gifts, patronage, awards—all dispensed with realism and fairness. The seeker realizes that money is two-faced—dark and light—and decides to go with the light side.

Reversed Meanings. This reversal indicates carelessness with money or other material things. Wealth used stupidly. Envy and jealousy, especially of the wealth of others. When the card shows up badly placed, Gypsies remind one to beware of thieves.

SEVEN OF PENTACLES

Primary Meaning. The Seven of Pentacles signifies fortune, gain, and profit through long effort and hard work. But the figure knows when to rest, for he is working in harmony with physical nature instead of against it. There is a *temporary* rest indicated here. A cycle of moderate importance has been completed, but there are new things to be accomplished.

Secondary Meanings. There will be material success, but it is not yet fulfilled. The magical powers of nature are on the seeker's side. Good fortune is very possible, but inertia must be overcome. Once underway, the seeker has a great capacity for meaningful work, including hard physical work, because, to his way of thinking, matter and mind are spiritually united.

Reversed Meanings. There is cause for worry, anxiety, and melancholy regarding money or security. A project may be abandoned. A loan may not be paid. Money may be lost. Promising circumstances may end in failure. Delay and unfulfillment.

EIGHT OF PENTACLES

Primary Meaning. The Eight of Pentacles signifies the constant regeneration of new efforts on the material plane—new efforts at skill and craftsmanship. For this reason it has become the token of apprenticeship, training, and practice.

Secondary Meanings. A symbol of grace and skill in material affairs, but these are in the preparatory stage. A good card for those with talent, patience, and energy. The seeker has raw talent in the material arts. He may be a "jack-of-all-trades" but a master of none. Readers sometimes advise one to avoid too much concentration on immediate returns at the expense of long-term success.

Reversed Meanings. Voided ambition, vanity, a know-it-all attitude, failure. The misuse of skill. Wasted time. Dishonesty and injustice even with oneself. Too much concentration on immediate returns at the expense of long-term satisfaction.

NINE OF PENTACLES

Primary Meaning. The Nine of Pentacles symbolizes very high attainment and material fulfillment. An almost perfect situation regarding security, wealth, accomplishment, safety, and stability.

Secondary Meanings. There is experience and wisdom regarding one's material interests. There is stability in material affairs because of prudence, discretion, care, good taste, and order. This prosperity is the outcome of one's career or life work, and many times readers say it is enjoyed alone. The card has been called a token of "the solitary enjoyment of wealth," but the exact meaning depends somewhat on other aspects of the reading.

Reversed Meanings. Use caution: present stability will not endure for long. Loss. Danger from thieves. Deception, roguery, bad faith, voided project. Storms, with crops destroyed. Wealth that was gained from the misfortune of others. Nature expresses her anger.

TEN OF PENTACLES

Primary Meaning. The Ten of Pentacles represents perfection and completion on the physical plane. This card is the ultimate expression of the suit of Pentacles: wealth, property, security, family wealth, family tradition, great inheritance, a long and respected family line. One's roots. One's extraction.

Secondary Meanings. The strongest token of established wealth and family in the minor Tarot. A great household. Old money. Blood ties. Gain, riches, family matters, firmly established wealth and security. A very solid environment. A very strong token of prosperity.

Reversed Meanings. Family troubles. Lack of family ties. Trouble with an inheritance. Problems regarding legitimacy and lines of succession. The breakup of an estate. The restricting effects of a long family tradition. Loss through speculation and gambling. Some say to beware of burglary.

PAGE of PENTACLES

PAGE OF PENTACLES

Primary Meaning. The Page of Pentacles represents a stable, physical, and down-to-earth child. This page has a great deal of practical intelligence and has a fascination with the physical sciences. The Pentacles type enjoys sports and has a talent for any job where a hands-on approach is needed. He follows rules easily and seldom questions established authority. For that reason the Page is said to make an excellent student.

Secondary Meanings. A child who is very much in touch with the physical world. The child is said to be proud, diligent, realistic, careful, and honest. There are elements of conservatism, deliberation, thrift, common sense, order, study, application, and scholarship connected with this Page.

Reversed Meanings. A child who is lazy, idle, physically out of touch, dull, lacking in humor, wasteful, bigheaded, or spoiled. A lover of luxury. Sometimes an omen of unfavorable news.

KNIGHT OF PENTACLES

KNIGHT OF PENTACLES

Primary Meaning. The Knight of Pentacles represents a young adult whose concerns are physical, sensual, and material. The Knight is described as solid, trustworthy, patient, methodical, conventional, honest, and kind.

Secondary Meanings. This Knight is the defender of conventional ethics and traditions. He offers stability and security. He is financially well off and likes to surround himself with the good things in life. He is responsible and is a very good provider. The seeker may find that this Knight wants to offer help.

Reversed Meanings. The Knight has become the champion of an outmoded system. There is too much preoccupation with material gain and material things. He can be limited by old-fashioned and dogmatic views. He is smug, dull-witted, narrow-minded, and lacks foresight. He has little individuality, creativity, or imagination.

QUEEN OF PENTACLES

Primary Meaning. The Queen of Pentacles is described as an attractive, opulent, sensual woman who offers wealth, comfort, and security. She is practical, devoted, down-to-earth, dignified, generous, and friendly. She is domestic, enjoys material things, and likes to live in the grand manner.

Secondary Meanings. An earthy woman who enjoys all the good things in life. A woman who loves athletics, dance, or other physical activities. A wealthy and charitable lady. A woman with "greatness of soul." She has children and many friends. Her complexion can be extreme—that is, light or dark. She is a strong defender of conservative values. She has "earth mother" qualities.

Reversed Meanings. A woman who throws money away on opulence and display. She is unable to rise above dull materialism and is stingy and suspicious. She neglects duties and depends too much on others. She offers no security and trusts no one. But she cannot be trusted, either.

KING ᴏ̨ PENTACLES.

KING OF PENTACLES

Primary Meaning. The King of Pentacles represents a solid, reliable, and wealthy man. He is skilled in the practical, devoted to those he loves, and slow to anger. He is very much in touch with physical and worldly reality. He is often a businessman, a banker, an industrialist, or the owner of substantial property. A strong symbol of patriarchal security. A father figure.

Secondary Meanings. A good, methodical, cautious man. A wealthy man over 25 years of age. A friendly, steady, reliable married man. He brings great energy to practical matters. An enduring, energetic, capable manager. A steadfast, competent, thoughtful, trustworthy, and preserving worker. Constantly seeks new uses of common things.

Reversed Meanings. A man lacking in emotion: dull, insensitive, materialistic, and sometimes stupid. He is not bad tempered, but dangerous if offended. An old and vicious man. Vice, weakness, perversity, corruption, peril. As with all reversals, this one can be read as weaker than the upright meanings.

WHEN SIMILAR CARDS APPEAR IN A READING

One of the things that make Gypsy-style Tarot reading so picturesque and interesting is how similar cards are given special interpretations when they fall together in the same layout. The appearance of three Queens, for example, has a special meaning over and above what these cards signify individually.

In the Keltic method, for instance, the appearance of three cards in a row from the suit of Pentacles would symbolize something unusual. In the twenty-one-card Gypsy method, the appearance of three aces in the same triad would also denote something special.

Generally speaking, these repetitions are most powerful when the cards involved fall close together. But even when they are spaced apart, they should be taken into consideration. The method behind all of this is quite simple, and runs along the following lines.

When a reading—any reading—is dominated by a group of cards from the same suit, then that reading is said to be involved primarily with the things represented by that suit. If, for example, seven cards from the suit of Cups should fall, it means (in the Keltic method) that the reading—made up of just ten cards—is mostly involved with things of the heart: love, imagination, poetry, emotion, and artistic endeavor. If three of the four cards in the New Year's Eve reading (see page 156) were from the suit of Pentacles, we might suspect that the seeker had money on his mind.

The chances of an overwhelming majority of similar symbols appearing in a reading at the same time are slight, but it sometimes does happen. The list below tells us how many of these symbolic coincidences are interpreted.

Four Kings: The seeker will receive a great honor. Three Kings: A crucial and important consultation. Two Kings: An important meeting.

Four Queens: A great debate. Three Queens: A private meeting of women. Two Queens: Close and sincere friends.

Four Knights: The seeker will be involved in something very serious. Three Knights: A lively debate. Two Knights: A close, intimate friendship.

Four Pages: A sign of many children. Three Pages: Loud frolicking and disputes. Two Pages: General disquiet.

Four Tens: The completion of a great piece of work. Three Tens: A new and fortunate condition. Two Tens: An important change.

Four Nines: Something great will be gained with the help of a friend. Three Nines: A sign of success. Two Nines: Something will be gained.

Four Eights: Great health and material progress. Three Eights: Marriage. Two Eights: New experiences and knowledge.

Four Sevens: A sign of great fortune, but with very deep secrets. Three Sevens: Joy and wisdom. Two Sevens: Good news.

Four Sixes: Great happiness and abundance. Three Sixes: Love and harmony. Two Sixes: A beautiful friendship.

Four Fives: Watch your luck. Uncontrolled activity. Three Fives: Tough determination in hard times. Two Fives: Uncertainty.

Four Fours: A person of great logic, common sense, and reason. Three Fours: A subject of quiet reflection. Two Fours: Interest in material things and worldly pleasures.

Four Threes: Great reward and abundance as a result of a partnership or mating. Three Threes: A powerful symbol of growth and expression. Two Threes: A good harvest.

Four Twos: Powerful omen of a great new love affair or a reconciliation of lovers. Three Twos: Warmth and security. Two Twos: Great friendship and accord.

Four Aces: A very intense sign of good luck. Three Aces: A new beginning of success. Two Aces: Unity and individuality.

If it should happen that many symbols from the major Tarot dominate the reading, this betokens that the seeker has many powerful forces surrounding him that are somewhat out of his control. Major Tarot cards are more powerful than the minor. They place a serious and profound element in almost any reading. They have about twice the energy of most minor Tarot cards. And they are surely the most interesting, symbolically.

4

The Major Arcana

In covering the twenty-two cards of the major arcana, we shall prove as best we can that these cards and the *Book of Creation* are very similar in their symbolic content. In order to do this, we will wend our way through the deeper and more hidden meanings connected with each of these remarkable Tarots. The alphabetical letters appear in order, and the twenty-two parts of the universe (the astrological symbols) are considered according to our ancient key.

The literal meanings of the Hebrew letters are taken from the *Langenscheidt Hebrew-English Dictionary,* by Dr. Karl Feyerabend. The *symbolic* meanings of these letters are derived from *The Hebraic Tongue Restored,* by Fabre d'Olivet, with additional information derived from *The Tarot of the Bohemians,* by Papus, and *The Tarot,* by Mouni Sadhu.

The illustrations of the major cards are taken from several interesting and symbolically accurate old designs. These are very similar to Waite's modern pack and should cause the reader no confusion.

Once this material on the major cards is covered, we shall be fully prepared to learn several methods of Gypsy-style fortune-telling. These methods will be found in Chapter Six.

One • THE MAGICIAN

Symbolically accurate versions of the Tarot card called The Magician always resemble the figure shown in the illustration. This example of the first major card is taken from the Tarot of Marseilles, which was first published by B. P. Grimaud in Paris

THE MAGICIAN

in 1748. The Marseilles design is the most widespread in the world and is thought to be derived from much older fourteenth- to fifteenth-century patterns.

Although there are many styles of major Tarot design, the most usual and standard symbolism runs as follows: The Magician is pictured as an energetic young man with the tools of his trade before him on a table. He is sometimes depicted as a minstrel. Other times, he is shown as a cobbler, a juggler, a trickster, a conjurer, or, of course, as a magician. But the basic theme of the card always remains just about the same: a symbol of masculine creative energy, power, craftsmanship, and skill. Many times, the "tools" before him on the table are actually the secret symbols for the four elements of creation: the cup (water), the wand (fire), the sword (air), and the pentacle (earth). But many old cards, like the one shown here, don't display these clearly.

It is thought by some that the four tokens of creation were disguised in order to avoid further censure by the church, for they were generally known to be symbols of "pagan" magic. It is curious also that the floppy hat on his head is shaped very much like a lemniscate—the sign of eternal life and infinity among the ancients.

Cardreader's Meanings. The Magician is the card that represents a very spirited, strong, creative, and skillful man. He is also described as a craftsman who is virile, powerful, individualistic, agile, witty, productive, but especially creative. Because of all this, he is usually a great favorite with women—especially women who like "family men" and men who love children. Indeed, he is known to have an almost magical ability with women and an almost magical ability in the arts.

If this card should fall badly placed or upside down (reversed) in a reading, the meanings above are made much weaker or even opposite. We then hear of weakness, ineptitude, hesitation, abuse of power, failure or severe lack of imagination, and the like. In some positions, Gypsy readers interpret this card as an omen of divorce, but this must be read carefully.

Philosophical Meanings. If we interpret this symbolism more philosophically, The Magician betokens what we can call the active, energetic, masculine, creative principle. In fact, he is the symbol of energy and creation in the purest sense—that is, the sense in which the alchemists would have understood the icon.

The subjects of creation and energy have always been of the greatest importance in science, philosophy, and theology. Therefore, as we can see, the major Tarot begins by expressing itself as a "philosophical machine"—a guide to the mysteries of metaphysics.

But what of the relationship between this "Magician" and the *Book of Creation?* The first symbol treated in the *Book of Creation* is the first letter of the ancient picture alphabet, "Aleph." The letter Aleph, like The Magician, symbolizes male energy—the active, virile, creative principle. Because it is the symbol of creation, it is the first letter in the ancient alphabet.

The card considered here is also connected with this letter for numerological reasons, for Aleph is also the glyph for the number one. In symbolism, the numbers represent not only simple quantities, as in arithmetic, but also qualities—ideas—each with its own poetic meaning and force. "One" symbolizes the genesis, the beginning of all things. It is the number, we will remember, of creative power and individuality. It is also the primary number, that from which all the others have been evolved, the token for the beginning of new things and intense energy. And, of course, all of this connects perfectly with the spirit of the Tarot Magician.

The Magician is considered a very good card in a Tarot reading under most circumstances. This is especially true when he shows up in the right place in a woman's reading. This card, like all major cards, is much more powerful than any minor card that might resemble it—the King of Cups, for example—and will certainly dominate the general tone of the reading. Although the card is the symbol of energy and creation, it does not betoken the actual Creator. The Magician is not the symbol for God, although he may represent a lesser god (like the ox, which Aleph represents) in the ancient pantheon. The symbol of the godhead is reserved for another very special card.

The Magician is one of three cards that does not have an astrological sign connected with it. Instead, the letter Aleph is conjoined with the element of air. And air is the element of spirit.

Two • THE HIGH PRIESTESS

The High Priestess has always been a great favorite with Gypsy cardreaders. This is especially true when the card falls well placed in a man's reading. The symbol is usually pictured, as shown, as a young, attractive woman seated upon a throne. She wears a long flowing gown and holds a scroll half hidden in its folds. The illustration here is from the Rider-Waite Tarot, which was drawn and designed, with Waite's guidance, by Pamela C. Smith.

As shown, the crown of the Egyptian virgin goddess, Isis, is sometimes displayed upon her head, especially in Tarots made after the eighteenth century. But before that time, she is usually pictured with the crown of the papacy on her head. We can only imagine how shocking this symbolism must have been to many in the fifteenth century. In fact, many of the old cards take this revolutionary aspect one step further: the icon is called "La Papesse" (The Female Pope) instead of The High Priestess.

To the best of our knowledge, the name-change took place because a famous set of Tarot cards—the Visconti-Sforza Pack— was produced in the 1400's with a High Priestess included that

THE HIGH PRIESTESS

was, in reality, a startling depiction of a female pope. The figure pictured on that card was the then famous Sister Manfreda.

Sister Manfreda, a member of the Visconti family, was one of the first great feminists. In 1298 she was elected pope by an Italian Gnostic sect called the Guglielmites—a sect that believed a new age was coming in which women would be elected as popes instead of men. The typical fate of heretics befell her, and Sister Manfreda, although she tried heroically to defend herself, was arrested in 1300 and burned at the stake.

Later, when the Visconti family had a set of Tarot cards handpainted for them, they decided to remember Sister Manfreda, so they honored her memory by having her depicted as The High Priestess. The card still survives to this day, and it is now kept at the Morgan Library in New York.

Could the Viscontis have known the secret symbolic meaning of this card? It seems they must have. They chose exactly the right symbolic device with which to describe The High Priestess. Ever since, The High Priestess and The Female Pope have been intertwined.

As a result of this and many other stories, the spirit of The High Priestess' symbolism lived on; and this Tarot has been a special symbol of women's power and influence ever since.

The symbol was condemned by the church in the sixteenth century, and for a while the figure of Juno was used in place of The Female Pope or High Priestess in order to pacify the inquisitors. Many times, during religious persecution, pictures of Greek or Roman gods were substituted for some of the more controversial figures.

Cardreader's Meanings. In Gypsy fortune-telling, the meanings of this interesting symbol are further clarified. The High Priestess represents the spirit of woman in all aspects, but especially as the guardian of the house—the environment. She has been described as the mother of invention; very wise, intuitive, enlightened, reflective, receptive, and feminine. She may reveal hidden things to the seeker—things that bring strength and hope—and she can represent a strong source of encouragement for creative talent. The High Priestess will also be very secretive about certain things, and that explains the half-hidden scroll in her lap. She represents the feminine mystique, the anima; but above all, she is the reflective guardian of the house and the principle of triumph over materialistic and militaristic evil. She is sometimes described by Gypsies as the woman that all men see when they are in love; and many times they regard The High Priestess and The Magician as a symbolic married couple.

When the card is reversed or badly placed, the meanings are weaker or sometimes the opposite. And this could indicate shallowness, conceit, surface knowledge, dullness, gossip, disregard for the environment, and the like. In the reversed position, all extremely good cards except two can, of course, be extremely bad. But that kind of interpretation must be left to the reader.

Philosophical Meanings. When interpreted philosophically, The High Priestess symbolizes the feminine, reflective, protective principle—the house of the cosmos. This principle, as understood by the ancients and the alchemists, is *space itself*. Space being the ultimate "house" in which we all live.

Just as The Magician represents energy, so The High Priestess represents space—to the ancients, the great feminine force which controls the very source of life; the passive element in the Creator. Her energy is the reflected light of the moon as contrasted with the direct light of the sun.

This Tarot card connects very well with the symbolism contained in the *Book of Creation*, for the second letter in the old picture alphabet is "Beth," a symbol for the feminine, reflective, creative principle. Pictorially, "Beth" represents a house or a dwelling, and as a spoken word, it means "house," "dwelling," or "tent."

Most translations of this ancient book also connect the letter Beth directly with the moon. And the moon is the "planet" that pertains most strongly to the house and to the home—to relations with women, especially the mother. The letter Beth also represents the number two, the symbol of duality, receptiveness, and reflection. One engenders two, and two creates three. Two is the number of the binary, duality; hence the idea of reflection.

The High Priestess symbolically represents many of the aspects of the great mother goddess who was worshiped for tens of thousands of years by the ancient peoples and who, in many respects, is still worshiped until this day. In the Tarot, the great mother goddess is so important that parts of her total personality are divided up and shared by the symbolism of at least five different cards, this card being the first. The High Priestess card represents the great mother in her purest sense, but the next card represents her as a goddess of fertility.

Three • THE EMPRESS

The Empress is usually pictured as a seated, pregnant figure who is noticeably younger than The High Priestess. She usually wears a secret sign of trinity; here, it is her three-pointed crown. Some cards display her with the wings of an angel, as in the illustration, and others show her surrounded by the fruits of a good harvest—bundles of grain and ears of ripe corn.

The example here is from the Tarot of Oswald Wirth—a simple but beautiful rendition designed in about 1927 from much older patterns.

The Empress is the third of the major Tarot cards, and this number signifies trinity: the father or thesis (The Magician); the mother or antithesis (The High Priestess); and now the child or synthesis, The Empress. This sequence represents the ancient conception of the triad at its plainest level.

l'Impératrice

Cardreader's Meanings. When The Empress falls well placed in a reading, this can betoken the birth of a child or the coming of a child. Fruitfulness in all its aspects is symbolized here. The Empress represents fertility. She is the guardian of childbirth and motherhood; and she signifies abundance, good harvest, plenty, material well-being, fecundity, and physical pleasure: all that is good when living in harmony with nature. Gypsies say she reigns with great love over all that has been born, all that lives now, and all that will be born in the future.

When the card is reversed, it can have the opposite meanings. Some of these would be sterility, poverty, maternal tyranny, unwanted or neglected children, and the like. In fact, in earlier times an extreme reversal of this card was looked upon with horror by many because this "falling" was an omen of barrenness, famine, or plague. Thank goodness, extreme reversals do not take place very often in serious readings.

Philosophical Meanings. From a more abstract point of view, The Empress represents all the material world. For she is *matter*—nature in its material sense. She is the daughter of The Magician (energy) and The High Priestess (space), and she is the door by which we leave the spiritual world and enter the physical world for a while: the womb.

She is tied up with the superabundant creative forces of nature, and her concerns are essentially on the physical plane—the manifestation of the great mother goddess in our "real" world of everyday concerns: the microcosm. When we consider The High Priestess, the emphasis is on the word *goddess,* but with The Empress, the emphasis is on *mother.*

The third letter treated in the *Book of Creation* is "Gimel." As a pictogram, Gimel represents the birth canal, the womb, and other tunnel-like transporters of material things. The ancient book connects this letter with the planet Venus; and Venus is the symbol of fertility, love, pleasure, and physical wealth. Venus is the morning star; she symbolizes feminine youth, love, and sensuality in all its joys and aspects; but above all, the planet signifies fruitfulness, harmony, and youthfulness just as does the Tarot we now describe.

Gimel is also the sign of trinity—the number three—and this number, you will remember, represents a synthesis: the fruits of a partnership or mating. When taken as a whole, the first three Tarot cards represent a triad—a trinity—and the nature of the mysteries of the trinity was one of the most important philosophical questions in ancient times. The early Christian church was sharply divided into a number of warring sects because of arguments over the nature of the Trinity. This was especially the case at Alexandria in the first few centuries after the time of Christ.

When fortune-telling, the traditional Gypsies lay out the Tarot as seven sets of triads plus one very special card which crowns the entire layout at the exact center—the top of the fourth triad. The symbolic layout of the first three cards runs somewhat as follows:

Father	Mother	Child
Energy	Space	Matter
Unity	Duality	Trinity
Creation	Reflection	Generation
Individual	Extension	Community
Thesis	Antithesis	Synthesis
Positive	Negative	Neutral

Four•THE HIEROPHANT

The first triad deals with some very metaphysical concepts, but the second views things from a more down-to-earth level.

The Hierophant—or "The Pope," as he is sometimes called—is portrayed as a distinguished-looking older man seated upon a throne. Many times he is shown holding a key, or a secret symbol for a key. This is true on most of our oldest reference cards. The incorrect number on this card derives from the Catelin Geofroy sequence.

The illustration shown here is from the more modern Tarot of Oswald Wirth. Two priestly ministers or followers usually kneel before The Hierophant; and although he wears the crown of the papacy, it is doubtful that he really represents the pope at all. He is more likely a true hierophant. *Hierophant* in ancient Greek means "discloser of sacred things." The ancient hierophant was not necessarily a peaceful man. He would fight, or even wage war, in order to protect his temple.

Cardreader's Meanings. The Hierophant symbolizes a member of the established church or a wise counselor of some kind. He is usually defined as a priest, minister, rabbi, or psychological counselor these days; but he can also be a professor, brother, or teacher, especially if the subject is connected with philosophy or theology. Gypsies describe him as a good advisor, a very ethical man who will give the comfort of religion, inspiration, and help. He symbolizes the ruling power of external religion and philosophy, especially in the more conservative forms. The card may also betoken brotherhood, militant guardianship of the church, morals, mercy, sanctuary, advice, and protection by the church.

When the card is badly placed or reversed, we get such interpretations as bad advice, distortion of holy teachings, unorthodoxy, nonconformity, superstition, heresy, renunciation of the church, slander, and withheld information. The card can then portray a very unconventional religious leader or a power which runs against established church authority.

Philosophical Meanings. The Hierophant is the protector of the church or temple. In a fuller sense, he is also the protector of all established theological and philosophical knowledge, especially as it is related to ethics. He holds the keys to the door of the sanctuary; and in ancient times that sanctuary was the storehouse of all accepted and valued knowledge. The church, the school, and the library were all part of the same thing; and that entity was guarded by the priesthood.

The fourth letter treated by the *Book of Creation* is "Daleth." Daleth symbolizes a door-latch. This is interesting when we note that several of the oldest Tarot references portray The Hierophant with a key in his hand.

The planet connected with this letter is Mars. Mars represents the willingness to defend, i.e., courage. It also signifies enthusiasm and passion that is seldom discouraged. It is the planet of builders, and betokens a strong sense of brotherhood. But there is an aspect of conservatism, intolerance, and quick temper associated with Mars; and its connection with war and defense is well known.

Daleth is the fourth of the ancient picture-letters. The number four is represented by the cube or square. It is the symbol of logic and reason in its more "solid" sense. Four is the token of philosophy at its practical and conventional level—theology in its conservative form.

Five • THE EMPEROR

The Emperor is typically shown as a proud, authoritative-looking man who sits on a massive throne. Many times the head of a ram (symbol of Aries) or a black eagle is clearly inscribed on it. The symbol of the eagle is the heraldic stamp of the Visconti-Sforza family.

The card example pictured here is from the Oswald Wirth pack, and it is typical of most accurate Tarot designs.

Cardreader's Meanings. This icon represents a powerful political leader or other authority who is friendly and democratic; but in contrast with the last card, here the emphasis is on power rather than philosophy. In a fortune-teller's layout, the card can betoken a stalwart defender of freedom, political protection, government, democratic checks and balances, political fairness, open forum, or authority in general. An authoritative figure with influence could be put at the disposal of the seeker, and this could be a strong fatherly or commanding person. In fact, many times the symbol represents the seeker's father.

The card, when well placed, will always represent the good king or benevolent leader; but when the symbol is reversed, its meanings are weaker or the opposite: harsh dictatorship, loss of power, fear of authority, weakness, fear of the electorate, and the like.

Philosophical Meanings. While the card called The Hierophant represents the church, this card represents the state. While the former is concerned with knowledge of the world, the latter is concerned with the power to control the world.

It is interesting that the card called The Hierophant (the church) falls before the card called The Emperor (the state). This is very much in line with ancient thought, because it hints that the church should "come in front of"—take precedence over—the state. In those early times, there was a saying: "As above, so below." This meant that the everyday world here in the microcosm should be a mirror image of the divine world— the macrocosm. The attitude was that political organizations should "copy" the organization of the gods above. And who should know more about this divine organization than the chief priest?

Many of the early Egyptian governments strove for fairness and open forum; and we see this strongly reflected in many of the myths about the political organizations of the ancient Babylonian, Egyptian, and Greek gods, among others. In ancient times, the idea of a thoroughly democratic but extremely powerful church where the congregation (women included!) actually controlled all aspects of its teachings was a completely Gnostic idea. But the attitude was considered dangerous and heretical by the founders of the early Christian church.

The fifth alphabetical picture-letter found in the *Book of*

Creation is "He." This symbol is known to represent all that is connected with freedom, openness, freshness, free breathing, and easy access. In fact, when pronounced, this letter meant "window" until modern times.

The ancient book conjoins this letter with the sign Aries. There is no sign that better describes the strong, freedom-loving, political man, for Aries is assertive, dynamic, aggressive, enterprising, scrappy; and he does not like to be outdone by anyone at anything.

The symbolism of this second triad is interesting because it compares the locked door (the key) of the holy man with the "open door" of the political man. The symbolism suggests that it is necessary for the holy man to keep the door of his sanctuary protected, much the same as the Ark of the Covenant was protected in ancient times. The political man, on the other hand, is a public figure. He must keep his door open and his services available to anyone who wishes to speak.

Six • THE LOVERS

The usual symbolism here consists of a young man flanked by two attractive women, and each woman seems to be trying to catch the man's attention while he remains undecided between them. Cupid aims his powerful arrow just above the main group.

The delightful, pixielike figures shown here are from the Oswald Wirth Tarot; all of the symbolism displayed here remains faithful to the much older Marseilles-style patterns.

Cardreader's Meanings. When this card falls in a reading, it is usually interpreted as an indication that an important choice must be made in the area of love, beauty, desire, romance, or the like. Some describe The Lovers as the symbol of sacred versus profane love. The seeker must make a choice, and it's not necessarily easy. Sometimes this choice is between mother and wife or husband and father. Other times, this choice is between wife and mistress or husband and lover.

At times the card simply betokens love or attraction itself— something that binds all of us together as human beings—but there is always an element of choice. Gypsies also give this card

VI

l'Amoureux

the general meaning of "beauty in both body and soul."

As one might expect, this card is a great favorite with fortune-tellers. It is the most powerful symbol of love in the Tarot, its energy being even greater than that of the Two of Cups defined earlier.

When reversed, the card can signify bad choice, infidelity, danger of moral lapse, divorce, severe temptation, quarrels, or a bad marriage.

Philosophical Meanings. All of the major cards can be read according to their philosophical meanings, for these just make the symbolism richer and more interesting. Here, the icon represents love, of course, but also aesthetics itself: the study of the nature of beauty in both the physical world and in the arts. According to this interpretation, the naked woman on the card represents the beauty of the *eye* (profane love), and the clothed woman who is speaking to the man represents the beauty of the *ear*—the intellectual and poetic sphere (sacred love).

The sixth letter covered in the *Book of Creation* is "Vav." And Vav is the symbol of something that binds things together, like a fastener or hook. Vav also has the secondary meanings "eye" and "ear." And when all these meanings are combined, we come up with the idea of visual art (eye), music and poetry (ear), and love (binder)—a very obvious use of ancient symbolism.

The sign connected with this alphabetical symbol is Taurus. An earth sign, Taurus is mainly connected with joining, mating, physical pleasure, comfort, and stability. In ancient times, Taurus was also the sign of all lovers; it was the sign of springtime.

But, most interesting, the present triad—(4) The Hierophant; (5) The Emperor; and (6) The Lovers—symbolizes three of the most important divisions in ancient and modern philosophy. These are ethics (and its connected theology and metaphysics), political philosophy, and aesthetics.

Seven • THE CHARIOT

The Chariot displays "an erect and princely figure" (as Waite described him) who stands in a chariot that is being pulled by two horses or two sphinxes. (Sphinxes on some Tarot cards became popular after Court de Gebelin advanced his idea about the Egyptian origin of the major cards.) The charioteer usually holds a wand of authority or a sword in one hand and wears the crown of a monarch. Most of the older reference cards display him holding a sword or other weapon.

The example here is from the Oswald Wirth Tarot; it shows the sphinxes very clearly.

Cardreader's Meanings. When The Chariot falls well placed in a fortune-teller's layout, it is viewed as a symbol of victory and triumph with justice. And although the card has a military tone, it is the icon of great brilliance, speed, mental activity, effort, conquest, and victory that will come through hard intellectual work. Like all of the cards in the suit of Swords, his sword represents conflict, duality, harsh-decision-making ability, and intellectual courage. But this major card is more powerful than any of the cards in the minor Tarot.

Sometimes Gypsies interpret this card as a sign of good news, especially if the good news has been brought speedily. In fact, the card can denote the speedy distribution of any information. Other times, they view this card as the symbol that represents a military commander or heroic person. But when the card is

le Chariot

reversed, the interpretation can become very grim: "Out of the strong comes forth sweetness and from the weak the bitterness of misery." A reversed Chariot is also described as an omen of unethical victory, uncontrolled passion, hot temper, intellectual laziness, and egomania. Certainly not a pretty picture.

Philosophical Meanings. When viewed more abstractly, the total symbol is difficult to describe. It represents intellect, primarily, but also a complex of active, male, mental, daring, speedy, victorious, and warlike components. And it has been suggested with good evidence that the card represents Alexander the Great himself (after whom the city of Alexandria in Egypt was named).

Above all, the card seems to signify a sharp intellectual division, and the duality causes great mental conflict. It is as if the symbol represents a great war which the individual must wage against himself in order to gain a kind of perfection . . . discipline, perhaps. At any rate, the symbol is considered to be primarily masculine and is sometimes said to denote "masculine intelligence"—hence the strong military aspects.

The seventh picture-letter covered in the *Book of Creation* is "Zayin," meaning "sword" or "dagger."

The astrological sign connected with Zayin is Gemini. Gemini

primarily represents great conflict on the mental plane. It is usually described as positive, airy, dual, masculine, and violent. Gemini types love to spread news very quickly, and they love to travel with great speed. People with this sign are reputed to know a little about everything, and they like very much to communicate all that they have learned. It has been said the best description of the Gemini type is the sentence "I think."

Eight • STRENGTH

Here, a frail but attractive young woman tames a ferocious lion without the slightest sign of fear or stress. Over her head is a lemniscate, which in some cases appears as a hat (as in the earlier illustration of The Magician). The example illustrated is from the Rider-Waite Tarot.

Called "Strength" in most English-speaking countries, this Tarot was called "La Force" in the early French versions.

Cardreader's Meanings. Basically, this card signifies woman's power to calm and domesticate—her ability to communicate with animals and nature. Other common attributions are: the higher controlling the lower; mind controlling matter; animal passion controlled; and the ability to calm people during a disaster. The ideas of courage, faith, confidence, patience, sensitivity, and willpower also come into play when the card falls in a reading.

If reversed, we get such interpretations as lack of courage, lack of control, abuse of power, panic, coarseness, cruelty to animals, and of course, an antidomestic attitude.

Philosophical Meanings. As with The Chariot, the symbolism here is not easy to describe, but the symbolic complex runs along these lines: courageous, female, compassionate, domesticating, faithful, communicating, controlling, high-minded. The ancient Greeks had a word that best describes this combination: *sophia. Sophia* was also considered a female principle. Perhaps "intuition" is one right word to use here, and also a kind of "female intelligence" (or wisdom) has been suggested. *Sophia* is also the Gnostic word for "mystical knowledge."

Since this card is the antithesis of the last, the kind of intelligence described here is exactly opposite that symbolized by The Chariot, i.e., opposite of the male, active, brash, militant, logical, and the like. In the Strength card, beauty simply tames the "dangerous" beast; she does not find it necessary to conquer or destroy him.

The eighth letter, "Cheth," is the symbol for a barrier, such as one that keeps and protects domesticated animals. The zodiac sign conjoined with this picture-letter is Cancer, the sign that represents possession and retention, domestication and motherhood. A major stellar cluster in Cancer is Praesepe, which symbolizes a stall, manger, or pen for animals. Cancer signifies sensitivity, sympathy, empathy, and maternal care. Usually described as home-loving, tenacious, and imaginative, Cancerians often are nature lovers and researchers.

Nine • THE HERMIT

If the first two cards in this triad, The Chariot and Strength, denote mental brilliance on the one hand and mysterious *sophia* on the other, we can imagine an individual who *combines* these

"male" and "female" principles (thesis and antithesis) and forms from them a synthesis greater than the parts it comprises. Such an individual—even if he or she only made the attempt—would be considered on the road to spiritual mastery, for combining all of the most impressive things about The Chariot symbol and all of the most beautiful things about "La Force" would give to us an avatar, a true master, a messianic figure.

The Hermit is such. This is shown, as illustrated in Oswald Wirth's Tarot, by the light he holds and the symbol of "serpent power" at his feet.

Cardreader's Meanings. When this card falls in a Gypsy's reading, it will signify the mystic power of the sage. He, unlike The Hierophant, is more than just a philosopher: he is a true visionary mystic who can initiate one who seeks a road to enlightenment. He has been described as the wise elder who gives silent counsel and protection to the initiate. The card can betoken wise counsel, prudence, initiation, and mastery as it relates to almost any higher study. There will always be emphasis on the words "prudence," "great care," and "circumspection."

When the card is reversed, opposite meanings like rejection

of wisdom, irrational fear, ignorance, and refusal to follow sound advice are given instead.

Philosophical Meanings. The primary meaning is direct mystical knowledge—*gnosis,* as some ancient thinkers have called it. The Hermit is, above all, the mystic. Most times he is shown with a snake or serpent near his staff, a symbol denoting "the knowledge of good and evil" because of the famous biblical story. The light The Hermit holds symbolizes the gleam of enlightenment. The heavy stick he carries betokens readiness and protection.

In the Middle Ages, the mysterious-looking Hermit was replaced on most "polite" cards by the image of an aging priest who peered into an hourglass; this was subtitled "Old Father Time."

The ninth letter in the Hebrew alphabet is "Teth," which symbolizes a snake or a serpent, primarily; but it also has a secondary meaning, and that meaning is "protector." Teth is conjoined with Leo; and Leo, since ancient times, has always been called "Leo, the bringer of light," for it is the sign of cosmic splendor. Good qualities, once obtained from Leo, are never lost; and it is the token of great will, great faith, ritual, ostentation, leadership, and fiery love.

The Hermit is the ninth card of the major Tarot. Nine is the number that symbolizes the summing up of all the previous symbolic forces. It signifies attainment on all three planes: physical, intellectual, and spiritual. In the ancient numerology, only one number is more nearly perfect, and that is the number ten—the number of our next card.

Ten • THE FOOL

The symbol called The Fool is the most important part of the entire Tarot. Although it is one of the twenty-two major cards, it stands in a class completely by itself. The icon usually displays a simple fool, a court jester, a beggar, or a clown who has a look of innocence and charm about him.

Many times he is shown trudging along the road with a carefree smile on his face while a dog or other animal bites at his leg. In the beautiful version of A. E. Waite shown here, The Fool is about to walk off the edge of a cliff, but he shows no sign of

O

THE FOOL.

care or concern. Waite has convincingly managed to symbolize the most secret and subtle things about the true meanings of this icon.

Cardreader's Meanings. When this card falls in a reading, it signifies that the seeker must be especially loved by God and that he or she is surrounded by the best of spiritual forces. The card is said to represent the beginning of all creativity and to symbolize the ultimate in every sense. A seeker with The Fool's nature will rebel against many of the established patterns of society and try to live exactly as he sees fit. For this reason, the card is often read as a symbol of nonconformity and great individuality, much the same as the card called The Magician.

There is no reversal of the Tarot called The Fool, and the card cannot be badly placed in a reading. Indeed, it greatly improves the whole nature of any reading.

Philosophical Meanings. As we can see from the diagram on p. 15, the symbol called The Fool crowns the entire major Tarot design at its symbolic center. This is only fitting, considering the great symbolic importance of this card. The design is really interesting because it tells us something about the very basic theology of the Tarot's ancient designers.

The tenth letter treated in the ancient book is "Yod." Yod is the picture-letter that signifies a fully open hand—a Hebrew-Egyptian symbol for the ultimate, the eternal, the spiritual, and the infinite. Yod is the most important letter in the ancient alphabet, and it is considered the one from which all twenty-one others are made.

The *Book of Creation* conjoins the letter Yod with the astrological sign Virgo; and Virgo is primarily the symbol of the immaculate, the pure, the untouchable, and the perfect. In ancient times, Virgo was pictured as a virgin who held in her hand a green branch, an ear of corn, or a grain flower. She was directly connected with the Egyptian virgin goddess, Isis, and with the idea of an immaculate conception of a messiah. In fact, the ancient Hebrews called the sign Virgo *Beth-Lehem,* which means, "house of bread."

Once we combine all of the symbolism, it becomes apparent that the Tarot's ancient inventors had some very definite and interesting ideas about metaphysics and theology. First of all, we see that the Creator stands alone—there is no group here—and that indicates a belief in one god: monotheism. Second, we notice that the symbol is completely removed from the remainder of the Tarot design; this implies that the Creator is greatly superior to and far above us. In other words, the Creator is eminent as opposed to being immanent (down here conjoined with us, dwelling at the inmost heart of nature). And third, we notice that there is a great deal of emphasis on the purity, unknowableness, infinite perfection, and immaculate nature of the Creator. It is as if the designers of the Tarot were trying to tell us that the true nature of the Creator is beyond our ability to comprehend, no matter how hard we might try.

Of course, all of this sounds like very polite, acceptable, and conventional modern Western theology. In fact, it seems to place stress on certain rather sophisticated points. And from this viewpoint, there is thus far not a drop of heresy involved.

But let us continue.

XVIIII

le Soleil

Eleven • THE SUN

The card called "The Sun" is the happiest-looking symbol in the major Tarot section. It usually displays two joyful and carefree children who hold hands under the friendly rays of a huge noonday sun. Drops of sunlight that look very much like Yods (symbols of the ultimate) fall upon the children from the sky. This card comes from Oswald Wirth's Tarot.

Cardreader's Meanings. When The Sun falls in a fortune-teller's layout, it is interpreted as an image of great joy, for The Sun brings intense happiness of all kinds. It is the symbol of life itself, of vitality, vigor, excellent health, warmth, and great security. Sometimes, at its higher levels, it is considered the symbol of universal radiance or divine light. Gypsy readers at times explain this card in mysterious terms. A. E. Waite gave a hint of this when he described the card as signifying "the transit from the manifest light of this world to the light of the world to come."

This Tarot symbol is very powerful. It is never reversed or badly placed. It cannot be weakened or affected by other, bad, cards. Like The Fool, this image radiates a warm, joyful aspect onto the entire reading.

Philosophical Meanings. Up to this point, the Tarot symbols have expressed only two points of view that could be considered "heretical" in the medieval sense of the term. In the first triad, the universal creative trinity contained a female element in the godhead; and in the third triad, the ultimate form of enlightenment (again, a mixture of male and female principles) is a kind of personal *gnosis* that is connected with "serpent power."

But now we come upon a section of the Tarot, the fourth triad—the crowned triad—which expresses a clearly ancient and clearly "heretical" religious conviction: *worship of the sun.*

The card called The Sun rests at the exact physical center of the ancient Tarot design. And it rests just beneath the crown of the entire layout. That crown is the disguised and secret symbol for the one ultimate, perfect, unreachable Creator.

The eleventh picture-letter is "Koph." Koph is the symbol for a half-opened human hand—the symbol of something slightly less absolute than Yod (the fully opened hand); and the symbol for something very powerful but finite and comprehensible.

In the *Book of Creation*, it is said,

> He caused the letter Koph to predominate in fertility, placed a crown upon it and combined it with the others. He created with them the Sun in the Universe, the fourth day in the year, and the left eye in the male and female person.

In all of astrology, the sign of the sun is the most powerful and dynamic. For this sign betokens the vital energy which enables life itself and all of life's activities. The sun expresses our consciousness, our egos, our drive for life, our self-esteem, and our security.

I have provided an illustration of the fourth triad—the crowned triad of the Tarot—so that some theological convictions of the system's ancient inventors might be clarified.

As we can see, The Sun rests just below the secret image for the unknowable Creator, The Fool. But, according to the designers of the Tarot, since the actual Creator is so unfathomable and untouchable; so awesome in its perfection; and so pure we can

The fourth and central triad of the Tarot, with the card called The Fool crowning the design. Note that the symbol for Divine Justice and the symbol for the Virgin Mother Goddess are located very close to the Sun God. These cards are from the Tarot of Oswald Wirth. (*Photo by Steven P. Stepak.*)

never know it, approach it, or understand it, we must look to something in the universe that is a direct *reflection* of the ultimate—a just slightly lower manifestation of the Creator. Many of the ancients chose the most obvious and concrete thing: that great orb above them, the sun. They worshiped the sun's life-giving light and heat.

Eventually the sun became a symbol of a higher light—the ancient Hebrews called it the *ain soph aour* (the pure limitless light). Akhenaton, pharaoh of Egypt c. 1372–1354 B.C., was the first monotheist. He believed the only god was the sun—Aton-Re. He rejected the traditional panoply of gods, closing their temples and having their names and figures removed from all possible monuments. Akhenaton devoted his whole life to trying to convince the Egyptian people that his one god, The Aton, was the only true god, and that worship of all others should be abandoned forever. And a few reliable historians think that his dedication even influenced Moses the Hebrew, several generations later. But just a generation or so after he died, all of Egypt returned to the older, mainline polytheistic religion that had endured there for thousands of years—the religion that included Isis, Osiris, Horus, and Amon-Ra.

Still, the religion of Akhenaton survived till the time of Alexandria, in the form of symbols. The most common image of Akhenaton was one of him with his wife Nefertiti (as a very young, happy, almost childlike couple), holding hands under a huge noonday sun. From this huge sun, rays of eternal life extend and touch the couple—pour a blessing on them. Each ray ends with the symbol "Koph," the symbol of the *half-open human hand*.

Akhenaton's religion even influenced the Bible; and sun worship influenced Greek, Roman, and eventually the Christian religions. The birthday of Sol Invictus was December 25—now celebrated as the birthday of the Son.

Twelve • JUSTICE

We view the familiar figure of Justice—a lovely young woman who holds her double-edged sword in one hand and the well-known set of scales in the other. Here, we see no blindfold. She views the world with both eyes wide open, and this is the exact style in most Tarot versions.

The illustration shown is from A. E. Waite's Tarot, which places the card as number eleven instead of number eight, the original number given in the Catelin Geofroy sequence. Interchanging card eight with card eleven was the only public change A. E. Waite ever made in the numeration of the Tarot; and as we see, it is very close to the sequence found here.

Cardreader's Meanings. When the Tarot card Justice falls in a reading, it is viewed as the symbol of fair dealing, honesty, integrity, balance, and equity. Many times, it signifies the triumph of the deserving side in a legal dispute or some sort of agreement reached by fair negotiation. Even marriage can be signified. The law is always involved; and to the seeker, this can be a card of

either hope or fear, depending on his ethical or moral position in the matter.

When the card is reversed, opposite meanings can be indicated: bias, legal injustice, lack of fair dealing, false accusations, bigotry, and the like. The reversal of the card, combined with other indications, can also mean involvement in a lawsuit, the loss of a lawsuit, or an impending divorce.

Philosophical Meanings. The figure of Justice is usually thought of as coming to us from the ancient Greeks. There she was the goddess Themis, who was the guardian of the infant Zeus. But this Greek goddess had an earlier Egyptian prototype, Maat, who was either the wife or the female equivalent of the famous god of justice Thoth—the god who, in the great judgment hall of Osiris, weighed the hearts of the dead with his well-known set of scales in order to test their worthiness. Like Thoth, Maat was concerned with weighing the truth and arriving at fair conclusions. The Greeks and the Hebrews, however, raised justice and the law to heights it had not previously reached in the ancient world, and that's probably why we see the figure of Justice resting so close to the supreme sun god in the Tarot design.

The Greek poet Hesiod, for example, wrote this extract on justice at about 700 B.C.

Lay up all this in your heart: give ear to Justice,
and wholly forget violence.
This is the way that Zeus has ordained for mankind.
Fish and wild beasts and the winged birds
shall eat one another,
for there is no Justice among them.
But to man he has given Justice,
the highest good of all.

For these reasons, Justice was always associated with the highest
God in the ancient pantheon, whether this be Zeus (derived from
a sun god), Amon-Ra, The Aton, or Jehovah.

It's also interesting that the number twelve should be connected
with this symbol, because that number was firmly connected
with justice in early times. The Romans, for example, so associated
this number with the law and justice that they took great pains
to publish their first great set of laws on twelve tables at around
450 B.C. When it came to the law, however, the Hebrews seemed
to have more of a preference for the number ten.

The twelfth Hebrew letter is "Lamed." Lamed, when used as
a picture-letter, signifies arms that are raised and extended in a
powerful posture to teach. Lamed as a noun means an ox-goad,
but when used as a verb, it means to "teach" or "instruct."

The *Book of Creation* connects this letter with the sign of
Libra (The Balance), and the symbolism involved with the
astrological sign Libra is remarkably similar to that involved with
our present Tarot card. For Libra is the sign of equality and
fairness, harmony and cooperation, balance and partnership,
tactfulness and peace.

It has been said that the watchwords of this sign are "I relate,"
and Libra is often equated with union and marriage. A perfect
Libra type would be the first protector of liberty, diplomacy,
graciousness, and liberality regarding justice and the law.

Thirteen • THE STAR

An undressed water woman pours liquid from two urns. She
pours water on the land, and she pours water back into its
source: a pond, a sea, or a river. She is full figured, and many
versions picture her as being with child. Behind her, we count

eight stars. These probably symbolize the eight planets known at the time. Early versions had only seven stars representing the seven planets known to the ancients.

The example illustrated is from the Tarot of Oswald Wirth.

Most early Tarot versions show a bird or ibis (symbol of fertility) perched behind the woman on a tree, and this has been taken up as the standard on most Tarot images of The Star. The Ibis is also the symbol of Thoth.

Cardreader's Meanings. The card is usually taken as a sign of very good luck and is many times interpreted by Gypsies in a rather mystical and sometimes vague way. It is primarily the image which represents *grace* itself. Grace in the sense of divine love and protection which is bestowed on the worthy seeker or initiate. The icon can symbolize many closely connected concepts: inspiration; imagination; new perception of mental and spiritual things; baptism and purification by water; hope, insight, mercy; a trustworthy, sympathetic, devoted woman; and bright prospects of all kinds. It seems the primary meanings are a complex of grace, hope, purity, and divine protection.

When the card is reversed, the opposite meanings apply. Some of these would be pessimism, doubt, loss of friendship, rigidity of mind, adultery, and fall from grace. This Tarot, however, is seldom read in the reversed position. It is just too good a card.

Philosophical Meanings. The thirteenth picture-letter covered in the ancient *Book of Creation* is "Mem," and Mem is the symbol of the Water Mother, of woman as the companion of man. When the letter is used as a spoken word, it means "water" or "sea." "Sea," in Latin, is *mare, maria*. In this connection, we may note that the early and medieval alchemists called water "the mother seed and the root of all minerals." And it is also interesting to note that many of the medieval poets and philosophers continually refer to Mary, the mother of Jesus, as "The Star."

The *Book of Creation* does not connect this letter with any sign or planet; instead, the letter is conjoined with the element of water.

With this card, we must deal with another aspect of the universal great mother goddess of antiquity. This symbol adds depth to what we have already discovered in The High Priestess, The Empress, and Strength. Here, Mem, The Star, The Water Mother—*maria*—are symbolic of man's subconscious realization that he evolved from the pure, cold, clear water—the sea. The Star represents the celebration of the life-giving and purifying properties of water. This is the true secret meaning of the high Gnostic and alchemical mystery: "immaculate conception." For the sea is immaculate, but yet it is the mother of us all. Man's gestation period in the sea lasted for hundreds of millions of years. We have not forgotten.

From this, we can see how the name "Maria" is directly associated with virginity and purity, grace and mercy. The sea is a kind, gentle amniotic fluid. And from this we can understand why baptism is widely accomplished with the use of pure cold water—for its purity, its sterilizing characteristic, cleanses away "original sin."

After thinking on the total symbolism involved here, the question arises whether there was a very early Christian influence on the pagan symbolism of the Tarot. If there was a Christian influence on the Tarot, it was surely an Alexandrian-Gnostic influence. The Gnostics were devout Christians, and they developed a system of symbolism like that described thus far in this book. There were all sorts of secret and very profound symbols associated with the main characters in the Christian Gospels— we know that from a close examination of the Nag Hammadi Codices and other Gnostic texts—and there were also secret symbols that represented ideas, convictions. The main sources of this symbolism were the sacred alphabet (especially the Hebrew), the signs of astrology, and the significations of numbers.

On the other hand, the Tarot is not an invention of orthodox, conventional Christians. There are just too many "primitive" and "pagan" elements here. No devout Christian of the sixth century (or of the sixteenth century) would tolerate a picture of Mary as a naked woman—pouring water from two chalices, located directly under an icon of the universal sun god.

This Tarot card was not banned in the Dark Ages because, by then, very few people, if anyone, really knew the import of its real meaning. No one had connected the mysterious, kneeling water woman there pictured with the mystical Water Mother symbol in the ancient biblical picture alphabet.

Fourteen • THE HANGED MAN

Here we view a young man who hangs upside down from a wooden gibbet that is made from freshly cut trees. There is no sign of pain or concern on his face; instead, he has an expression of calm detachment and control. His hands are tied behind his back and one leg is crossed behind the other.

Many examples of The Hanged Man picture the youth with a bright halo around his head, but this seems to have been added sometime after the seventeenth century. Many cards use a good deal of the color green on this icon; in fact, some display green leaves budding from the trees there pictured. The example shown here is from the Tarot of Marseilles, and again the number applied is wrong.

Cardreader's Meanings. When The Hanged Man falls in a Gypsy layout, it is defined as a symbol of sacrifice and great idealism. The image will signify intense nonconformity, surrender to higher wisdom, ethical passion, great courage, faith in the values of the spirit, self-sacrifice, and even martyrdom. A complete

THE HANGED MAN

reversal of the seeker's way of life can be indicated, for the actions and the beliefs of The Hanged Man are contrary to the established conventions of society and place him in an inverted position compared to social norms.

When the card is reversed, the usual opposite meanings can apply, and these have been described as absorption in physical matters, compliance with the status quo, resistance to spiritual teachings, and the like. Sometimes when the card is reversed but well-placed, it can signify that a suicide will be prevented.

Philosophical Meanings. Of all the symbols in the major Tarot, this one is the most pagan. Many groups of early people were convinced that trees were responsible for human fertility and, especially, male potency. They believed that pleasing the tree spirit was the only way to ensure a good harvest for the coming year. Each spring, a young boy would be hung on a green sprouting tree and killed as a sacrifice so the tree spirit would provide a good crop and strong new children in the year to come. As time passed and these people became more civilized, the awful sacrifice was toned down a great deal. The young boy was just hung on the tree for a while, and mock sacrifices were carried out by members of the congregation. The Tarot card we are now considering portrays that mock sacrifice perfectly.

Faint glimmerings of this tree worship—a natural religion for forest dwellers—still can be seen in our May Day celebrations and Green Man festivities—as well as at Christmas when we bring a green tree into the house and gaily decorate it.

The major tree sacrifice, of course, was Jesus'. Gnostic texts written by Valentinus and his followers well over fifteen hundred years ago use the vivid symbolism of the tree sacrifice in a remarkable way. In the *Gospel of Truth*, the writer describes Jesus on the cross as fruit on a tree, a new "fruit on the tree of knowledge" that yields life, not death:

> . . . nailed to a tree; he became a fruit of the knowledge [*gnosis*] of the Father, which did not, however, become destructive because it was eaten, but gave to those who ate it cause to become glad in the discovery. For he discovered them in himself, and they discovered him in themselves.

The *Book of Creation* adds some convincing elements to this symbolism, for there the fourteenth picture-letter is "Nun," which is the symbol for The Son of Man, for offspring, for the newborn child, for fruit. It is also the symbol for every living being that is brought into this world.

The letter Nun means "fish" (symbol of fertility), and the fish was the secret symbol of the early Christians—in fact, it was the symbol for Christ himself among both conventional Christians and Gnostics.

To further add to this complex of symbols, the *Book of Creation* conjoins this picture-letter with the astrological sign Scorpio, an ancient symbol of fertility, courage, determination, personal magnetism, healing power, and sensitivity. Scorpio was the sign of the heroic type who would fight to the death rather than surrender his principles.

As with the last card, The Star, we are tempted to identify the young sacrifice who hangs from the tree—The Hanged Man. Does this card secretly represent the crucifixion of the Savior? Or does it represent the sacrifice of an earlier mythological personage? These are difficult questions. Perhaps in the final analysis the card is meant to represent a higher symbolic archetype.

It is astounding that this image falls in the design right after the symbol for the universal virgin mother goddess—The Water Mother.

Fifteen • THE TOWER

This is certainly one of the most frightening major cards. Here, a huge tower is smashed by a bolt of lightning, and this bolt is tipped by an arrowhead. Two human figures fall helplessly from their stricken refuge while bits of the building fly in all directions.

The example here is from the Oswald Wirth Tarot, and displays the usual French title, "The House of God." Most cards, however, label this card as "The Tower" or "The Lightning-Struck Tower." The round objects pictured on the card are usually shown as drops of light in the older Tarot examples. They are probably the secret symbols of divine blessing: the Hebrew Yods mentioned earlier.

Cardreader's Meanings. Even Romany fortune-tellers have a difficult time with this card, because the basic meaning is catastrophe. The powerful symbolism of The Tower speaks very well for itself, and the secret significations of the falling sparks (Yods) may be more subtle. Some writers on the subject have given hints. Alfred Douglas, for example, quotes from an uncanonical saying of Jesus that sounds very Gnostic:

> He who is near unto me,
> is near unto the fire.

And Eden Gray gives a more familiar quotation:

> Except the Lord build the house,
> they labor in vain that build it.

The Tower has very strong positive meanings, but these have never been commercially published. A. E. Waite also gives a hint in his characteristic style:

> I agree rather with Grand Orient that it is the ruin of the house of life, when evil has prevailed therein, and above all that it is the rending of a house of doctrine. I understand that the reference is, however, to a house of falsehood.

When the card falls in a fortune-teller's layout, it usually signifies catastrophe, calamity, ruin, overthrow, disruption, and devastation that is the result of natural or supernatural forces, all of this an "act of God." The card sometimes betokens the overthrow of an existing way of life, but all of the stress and trouble will bring enlightenment in its wake. It is said that within one season the outcome of the disaster will pass, that all will adjust, and that happiness will return to the survivors.

When the card is reversed, the above meanings are weakened. Sometimes a reversal betokens domination by a tyrant, imprisonment, oppression, terror tactics, or inquisition, but all of this is temporary. In either position the card is very difficult to read because it is such a violently spectacular image. A good deal of tact and prudence should be used when attempting to interpret this symbol.

Philosophical Meanings. Some think the symbolism of The Tower may have developed as a result of the biblical story about the Tower of Babel (an actual structure in ancient Babylon). Others think it is a reference to the destruction of the Jewish temple just after the death of Christ. And still others think it symbolizes the ancient fear of Saturn's power to destroy entire cities. Tarot expert Bill Butler writes that every "Tower" card he has ever seen unmistakably implies divine, super-rational destruction.

The fifteenth letter in the Hebrew alphabet is "Samekh." Samekh is the ancient glyph of a bow whose string hisses—a powerful, destructive bow. (Note the arrowhead on the example.) And the ancient Cabala tells us that trembling and wrath are connected with this letter. The book conjoins the picture-letter with the astrological sign Sagittarius—The Archer. And to the ancients, Sagittarius was above all else the sign of illumination that pierces the mere illusion of matter. Ara, the second deacon of Sagittarius, was the sign that the ancient Greeks viewed as a symbol of ruin and utter destruction. Sagittarius is also connected with the old Hebrew *mara* and *aram*, again meaning utter destruction.

This astrological sign always represents places that are the highest in the land, and structures that rise higher than the surrounding territory. Sagittarius also signifies fire, places where fire has been, arrows, and spears. The sign is represented as an arrow and the section of a bow; and in that respect, it is identical to the picture-letter we are now discussing.

When we combine all of the very vivid symbolism, it is apparent that the Gypsy interpretation of the card and the ancient view of it are just about the same.

Most interesting, The Tower represents the antithesis of our previous card, The Hanged Man. While The Hanged Man signifies voluntary death, voluntary sacrifice of the self for the sake of higher convictions, The Tower, on the other hand, symbolizes involuntary death, destruction, and chaos over which we apparently have no control.

We have now reached the fifth triad in the Tarot design: The Hanged Man, The Tower, and The Devil. And this is called, by the cabalists, the triad of severity and power.

Sixteen • THE DEVIL

A horned devil with bat's wings stands perched on a heavy stone foundation. The figure has large breasts, and the almost naked body is rather feminine. Most Tarot packs picture a torch held in one hand and a lit candle in the other. At its feet stand two lesser horned creatures, each restrained by a loose halter around the neck that is fastened to the stone foundation by a metal ring or eye. This ring is an occult symbol which signifies worldly power, great wealth, and magical abilities. It is associated with the evil eye of black magic.

The example used here is characteristic of most Tarot versions. It is from the Tarot of Oswald Wirth.

Cardreader's Meanings. When the card called "The Devil" falls in a fortune-teller's layout, it is understood to signify bondage to material objects—gross materialism and all of its evils. The card also symbolizes lust for power, and cruelty, greed, promiscuity, and evil in general. Gypsies have been known to compare this card with the personality of the Marquis de Sade: it betokens the misery of the materialist who has lost his soul because of his relentless greed and his fanatical drive to gain power over others.

When the card is reversed, the meanings can remain the same but they are weaker: attachment to petty power, selfishness, bullying, spitefulness, and addiction to objects. Sometimes the card is said to indicate a dangerous repression of the instincts by an over-logical intellect. This is especially true when the card is reversed.

Philosophical Meanings. Like The Tower, the abstract meanings of The Devil symbol are very similar to those given by the Gypsies: bondage to the material world, and the weaknesses and evils involved therein. The total symbolic complex runs along these lines: materialism, gluttony, extreme practicality and logic, lust for power, conformity, bondage, and fearful obedience. In these respects, the card is very similar to what is signified for the sixteenth Hebrew letter. This picture-letter is "Ayin." The symbolic meaning of Ayin is a *material tie or bond*. According to D'Olivet, the letter signifies the bond with the material world through visual contact. (As a spoken word, the letter means "eye.") He also says the glyph expresses all that is crooked, false, perverse, and bad. This is interesting, because many commentators, including Gypsies, connect the sixteenth card with the "evil eye" of black magic.

Our ancient book conjoins this letter with the astrological sign Capricorn. Capricorn is the sign of the ambitious, the practical, and the materialistic. The sign has also been described—from the negative point of view—as being cold, conventional, relentless, autocratic, and power-hungry. Capricorn has been pictured as a goat with a fish's tail for thousands of years, and that is striking when we consider the symbol on our present card.

Whether the Tarot design spells out a definite ethical or moral doctrine is unknown. It certainly seems to, but interpreting the symbols morally is a tricky business. Symbols, of course, can mean many things to many people. For this reason, one must use care when trying to define moral or ethical values that might be conjoined with them. The one ethical doctrine that seems to show up over and over again in the Tarot is the doctrine of antimaterialism—a suspicion and distrust of extremely materialistic values. We know that the vast majority of Gypsies do not like to be tied down or controlled by materialistic considerations. Many cards in their minor Tarot preach against materialism. And there are very few traditional-style Gypsies who ever dream of investing their money in a "condo" or of owning a big fancy house in the suburbs. So, the question arises: Are the Tarot cards antimaterialistic, or do the Gypsies place an antimaterialistic overlay upon them?

From what we have seen here (with the ancient numbering), it seems certain that the Tarot itself takes an antimaterialistic moral and ethical stance. And for all we know, the Gypsies adopted their views—their style of life—because of an unforgettable ancient experience with the Tarot philosophy.

The three icons in the fifth triad—the triad of severity and power—can be treated as thesis, antithesis, and synthesis as follows:

The Hanged Man	The Tower	The Devil
Nonviolence	Violent overthrow	Fearful obedience
Martyrdom	Involuntary death	Practicality
Rebirth	Waste	Bondage
Spiritual growth	Decay	Lust for power
Sacrifice	Catastrophe	Material protection
Idealism	Nihilism	Materialism
Resurrection	Disintegration	Maintenance

Seventeen • TEMPERANCE

This Tarot card portrays a beautiful winged angel who pours the essence of life carefully from one chalice into another. The angel usually wears a magical symbol as a headpiece, and accomplishes the task at hand in a very graceful and balanced manner. While the figure is mainly portrayed as feminine, angels are usually neither male nor female.

This example, one of the most classic Tarot designs, is from the Tarot of Oswald Wirth. This complete set of cards can be found as illustrations in *The Tarot of the Bohemians,* written in 1889 by Papus. (The third edition of this book, by the way, is still available to the public from Wilshire Book Company of North Hollywood, California.)

XIIII

la Tempérance

Cardreader's Meanings. When the card called "Temperance" falls in a Gypsy reading it can signify such things as self-control, moderation, economy, and of course, all tempering influences. Sometimes, however, the card is read as a symbol for excellent communicating abilities, great partnerships, coordination, adaptation, accommodation, and good combinations of all kinds.

At still other times, the card is read as the symbol for time itself—the passing of time—time which heals all wounds and keeps volatile situations under control. On many occasions we hear of the time element in fortune-telling. A Gypsy, for example, might say that an important event will take place, but then go on to specify a time element. Most times, this is done with the use of the Temperance card.

The icon is the symbol of moderation, communication, and time because these three elements are the most important tempering influences.

When the card is reversed, the opposite meanings can apply. And some of these would be lack of communication, decadence, bad combinations, clumsy handling of situations, imbalance, volatile factors out of control, and of course, severe time problems of some kind.

Philosophical Meanings. Sometimes this card is grossly misinterpreted as being strictly anti-alcohol. But temperance in this case means moderation, not abstinence. Anyway, the true symbolism is more alchemical in nature.

The card denotes time, particularly in the way understood by the alchemists—Time, the *communicator* of the elements, energy, and mass; and Time, the great moderator and modifier of these primal elements. The angel here pictured is pouring the essence of life and creation gently from one chalice to the other, and she will do so for infinity.

The card called Temperance, at its highest level, symbolizes the *infinity* of time, of *eternity*. When the alchemists asked about the catalyst that tempers and conserves matter and energy by controlling these very powerful and volatile factors, the answer came back, *Time*. When we look at the angel's cups, we know the mixing of matter and energy will go on and on forever.

The seventeenth picture-letter is "Pe," the symbol for human communication—the mouth with the tongue included, the mouth uttering its thoughts. And the astrological symbol connected with this letter is the planet Mercury.

Mercury is, above all, the symbol of communication. It has been described as the link between spirit (energy) and matter in the universe. Its highest application is in the realm of pure reason, but it knows so much of both sides of a duality that it can never draw a final conclusion. Wherever Mercury is placed in an astrological reading, it signifies what is most thought about and what is most talked about. It is the planet that tends to temper the aspects of all other planets and influences.

Eighteen • DEATH

A homely, animated human skeleton mows down the field of humanity with his scythe. Many versions of the trump show the heads of kings, popes, and children at his feet. No one is spared.

As an image, Death has caused a unique and sometimes morbid fascination with the Tarot pack. It is easily the most famous and most widely misunderstood Tarot card.

The example pictured here is from the Marseilles Tarot. The symbolism shown is basically the same as that used on the cards five centuries ago. Sometimes the figure of Death rides on

horseback, but the basic symbolism of the image always remains clear and unmistakable.

Cardreader's Meanings. This card is seldom, if ever, used to indicate death in a seeker's reading. Traditional Gypsy fortune-tellers interpret the symbol primarily as the end of something—the conclusion of a matter; the finish of a certain stage. The trump can symbolize mortality itself: the fact that all things in this sphere must end. But of course, *life* is not the only thing that ends in this world. The card has been misinterpreted because of a wide popular misunderstanding about the true inner meanings of this—on the surface—primitive, frightening, and grisly symbol.

The icon, depending on how it is placed in a reading, can indicate a finish, an end, a very crucial change, and of course, mortality. Gypsies also don't give the prospect of death a completely dismal outlook as some others do. They don't give death the meaning of the void, the black sleep of nothingness; and this is very much in line with Gnostic and Hermetic thinking. One of the Gypsies' well-known sayings is:

> Man dies many times
> before his death.

Often Death is viewed as a "servant of mankind"—the dissolution of the old so that we might have something new; a symbol of changes, new ideas, and rebirth. In fact, the Death card can predict a crucial and important change in a person's life; that change will be determined by the other indicators in the reading.

When the card is reversed, it is viewed as an omen of lethargy and stagnation, inertia and sleep, resistance to change, hope destroyed, and petrification. But again, not as a card of death.

Philosophical Meanings. Our last card, Temperance, is the symbol for infinity in the sphere of time. With that symbol, we have all the time we can imagine. But this card, Death, is the symbol for mortality—for the end. Here, we are no longer in the domain of time. Our time has run out and stopped. But as far as we know, mortality is a necessary part of our existence on the physical plane; hence the Gypsy idea that death is, after all, a servant of mankind. For we cannot have life without death; we cannot have eternal spring; and we cannot have wakefulness without sleep.

At the abstract level, the icon is traditionally described as that principle in nature which must sweep away old life so that space might be made for the growth of the new. In a sense, all future life springs up from the rich loam of the past. Nothing is lost, nothing is wasted. Only the outer appearance of things—the form—changes.

The *Book of Creation* adds depth to the image. The eighteenth picture-letter covered there is "Tzaddi," and Tzaddi has the pictorial meaning of end, conclusion, finish, or limit. As a spoken word, Tzaddi means "hook for killing fish." Fish, as we discussed with The Hanged Man card, were the symbols of life, rebirth, and (eventually) the resurrected one. The fishhook is the symbol for the opposite: death.

The letter Tzaddi is coupled with the astrological sign Aquarius. Aquarius is regarded as the servant of humanity because he wills to tear down something old so that we might have something new. This symbolic image, like the image of Temperance, is associated with the coordination—the patient handling—of spirit and matter. While these are the primary meanings of the Aquarius symbolism, the sign can also denote times when sudden changes or explosive events can occur: unpredictable nature, revolutionary

THE MOON.

leanings, rebelliousness, and the like. Aquarius is always regarded as a friendly sign, a water bearer, a servant of mankind.

It may seem strange that a friendly, benign image like Aquarius should be connected with the card called "Death"; but this trump, we should remember, is not only a token of death.

Nineteen • THE MOON

This Tarot image displays a large, bright moon that radiates her light upon the terrain below. There we find a deep black pond out of which a lobster or crayfish is attempting to crawl. Before the lobster is a long, wending path that leads to greater heights. Farther along this path, we see two dogs or wolves baying at the moon. Still farther on this path, are two works of man: two large towers. Upon this whole scene, drops of light, the Yods, descend as a symbol of the guiding spirit.

The trump pictured here is from the Tarot of A. E. Waite and Pamela Colman Smith—The Rider Pack. It is typical of the exact symbolism used on the cards for over four hundred years.

Cardreader's Meanings. In fortune-telling, The Moon is mostly a card that denotes anxiety, worry, and unforeseen perils—fears, and sometimes very intense fears, in general. It can also betoken a crisis of faith—or deception, danger, hidden enemies, terror, withdrawal, evolutionary struggle and illusion. Gypsies say of this card that life is a bitter struggle and that evolution is a fearful and painful process. But the icon is complex, and dual in its aspect. Many times, when the card is well placed, it can denote encouraging psychic vision, calmness of mind, a strong, hardy soul, and a kind of universal compassion and comprehension: a kind of peace. Fear can be driven back to the place whence it was allowed to come.

When the card is reversed, it will signify that imagination has been crushed by conventionality, that there has been a failure of nerve: cowardice, fear of stepping beyond safe boundaries.

Philosophical Meanings. The major card called "The Moon" contains some of the most sophisticated and arcane symbolism in the entire Tarot system. As with The Star, we have here symbolism of life's evolution from the water. Here, primeval life struggles upward from the mysterious black pond, and the crustacean (the lobster, symbol of the lowly and the physical) begins the long journey on the path to more complex things. Later, we see the excited, howling mammals (symbols of the emotional); and still later we come upon the towers, the remnants of the tool- and monument-builders like man (symbols of the intellectual). Finally the path leads to the mountains near the upper moon world itself (symbol of the spiritual). All the while, this long, tortuous path gives us the impression of overcoming, of struggle, and of danger. Only the magical Yods, the tiny drops of light, rain down on us to give us hope and keep us encouraged.

The nineteenth letter of the pictorial alphabet is "Qoph." As a symbol, this letter denotes a sharp, double-sided stone axe—an instrument of defense. The glyph Qoph means "back of the head" when pronounced as a word; and when these symbolic ideas are combined, we get a good idea of what this ancient letter was used to signify.

In the *Book of Creation*, this picture-letter is coupled with the astrological sign Pisces. Pisces is the symbol for the silent, all-comprehending force that grants to every individual the power to act according to its development and capacity. Pisces personalities are also linked with fearfulness, withdrawal, submissiveness, spirituality, intense imagination, and dreaminess. The sign is represented by a pair of large sea horses or sea lions yoked together, who dwell in the innermost regions of the sea. And, to the ancients, this signified life after death. It has been said that Pisces types would advocate and teach a philosophical system that best prepares man for a life after death.

The sixth triad of the Tarot design can be laid out as thesis, antithesis, and synthesis in the following manner:

Temperance	Death	The Moon
Eternity	Finality	Anxiety
Immortality	Mortality	Illusion
Time	Timelessness	Evolution
Communication	Silence	Withdrawal
Coordination	Unity	Duality
Temperance	Acceptance	Fear
Motion	Rest	Self-protection
Grace	Fixity	Readiness

Twenty • THE WORLD

The World is the initial card of the seventh triad—the last triad in the major Tarot design.

Here, a youthful female figure seems to dance in the center of a large egg-shaped wreath. Her only clothing is a loose veil, and she always carries a wand in at least one hand. Around her, in each corner of the card we view the four symbols of ancient Hermetic science, the four elements of the sphinx: the angel, the eagle, the lion, and the bull. Later, these images would become the representation of the four living creatures in Ezekiel's biblical vision; and still later, they would become secret symbols in the Christian tradition for the four evangelists Matthew, Mark, Luke, and John.

In a sense, these four living creatures represent the four corners of the universe—the quarternary powers that ensure the stability of cosmic processes—and they are much the same as the four elements of creation: earth, air, water, and fire.

The example illustrated here is from the Tarot of Marseilles,

THE WORLD

and it is thought to be the most representative and accurate design of this particular trump.

Cardreader's Meanings. When The World appears in a fortune-teller's layout, it is defined as a token of the freedom to change, to move, to liberate one's self. The card also signifies progress of any kind, movement, travel, change of home, change of occupation, liberty, free will, worldliness, and a progressive, liberal, intellectual attitude.

Like some others, this card is a complex symbol and reads differently in different positions in the layout. Some of these various meanings can be: spontaneity, the discovery of new worlds, intellectual freedom, self-direction, cosmic consciousness, the perfection of the intellect, the perfection of the individual, and meanings along similar lines. But the basic symbolic complex is: free will, spontaneity, progressiveness, and worldliness.

When the card is reversed, opposing meanings will apply. And some of these are fear of change, strong attachment to one's place or occupation, inertia, fatalism, lack of vision, resistance to change, loss of momentum, failure of will, narrow-mindedness, self-imprisonment, and boredom.

Philosophical Meanings. The World is basically the card of freedom itself. It expresses the idea that humanity should be free to choose its own destiny. It signifies the conviction that there is a strong element of chance and spontaneity (indeterminism) in our universe. But this icon contains another element, and it is "worldly," progressive, open-minded, expansive, and intellectual. What is interesting about all of this is how Tarot symbolism at this point seems to become very modern and democratic in its outlook. In a sense, the sentiments it expresses don't seem to be very ancient at all. We must remind ourselves that Alexandria was a very cosmopolitan and intellectually oriented place around fifteen hundred years ago. Liberty, free will, and open-mindedness were everyday concerns of some of these ancient thinkers.

The *Book of Creation* clarifies the complex symbolism of The World somewhat. The twentieth picture-letter treated is "Resh." Resh was used to symbolize the free intellect, *the head of man in full profile,* man's movement and his progress. This letter is paired with the planet Jupiter.

Above all things, Jupiter represents the expansive principle: the will to grow and enlarge one's sphere of influence. It is the planet of worldliness and the token of the universalist. It denotes a progressive and optimistic attitude, a fearless and philosophical attitude, especially where change and new ideas are involved. In all these respects, it is nearly identical with the imagery on this card.

When the term *liberalism* is used in connection with this card, it seems to be used in its strictest sense—that is, a social and political philosophy that favors individual freedom and the rational consent of man as opposed to the authoritarian idea.

Twenty-one • THE WHEEL OF FORTUNE

Although the example illustrated is from the modern Wirth Tarot, the basic outline of the symbolism remains true to that used on cards dated as early as 1400. Here, we view a sphinxlike figure that sits upon a large wooden wheel. Two other odd-looking creatures—probably ancient Egyptian mythological figures—cling to the wheel also.

This was one of the major cards that prompted Court de

la Roue de Fortune

Gebelin to theorize that the Tarot—at least the major Tarot—must be of ancient Egyptian origin. De Gebelin's idea was not taken very seriously by the professional historians who followed him, because his evidence was very slender: only three cards of the twenty-two contained obvious Egyptian symbolism. No one, in his time, could prove that the Tarot was related to the Egyptian-Alexandrian *Book of Creation* or to the picture alphabet. Egyptology was then still in its infancy. De Gebelin was certainly on the right track, but more symbolic evidence than he provided needed to be unearthed.

Cardreader's Meanings. When The Wheel of Fortune symbol falls in a Gypsy's layout, it signifies the fate and fortune—the destiny—of the seeker. The Wheel, then, is read in conjunction with the other cards that surround it in the reading. This trump is traditionally connected with the ideas of fate, fortune, destiny, and luck; but all of these things are considered to be *predetermined,* fated. The image signifies the wheel of fate, the wheel of birth; and that the whole history of the seeker's life is somehow predetermined. Great cycles will be repeated, and what has been sown will be reaped. When the card falls in the upright position, the laws of fate are usually considered to be in the seeker's favor. But, if the card should fall reversed, we can expect a turn for the worse; that fate will be unkind; that life will be an uphill battle with long periods of difficulty and stress.

Sometimes the card is used to define the cyclic changes—the seasons—in a person's life; when surrounded by good cards and upright, the wheel works with us in a positive cycle. But, when surrounded by bad cards or reversed, the wheel works against us in a negative cycle. Again, as the Gypsies will insist, these positive and negative cycles are predetermined by the individual's fate.

Philosophical Meanings. The last card we covered, The World, symbolized the idea of indeterminism: freedom, spontaneity, accidental unfated events. But this card, The Wheel of Fortune, expresses the opposite: determinism, fate, destiny, cyclic events that must happen over and over again whether we want them to or not. This brings up one of the oldest and most heated arguments in all of philosophy: whether humanity has free will. According to the last card, we do have it, but according to the present one, we do not. Here, we are trapped on the unalterable wheel of birth and fate. Whatever happens to us in this life— whatever actions we may take—are all predetermined by the unfathomable laws of the universe. Our "luck" is not really luck at all. It has been laid out and planned for us. The only way to feel comfortable with our fate is to step back and take a wider view of the situation; to step back and view the whole wheel. We see that it eventually grinds everything down, assimilates everything, and prepares everything. It raises one thing up while it lowers another. It is like a mill of transformation, working on some high principle, which pulls and kneads us in a sometimes painful process in order to prepare a better dough for future bread. If we are unsatisfied, are we prepared to fight it? Or should we work in harmony with it? The Gypsies tell us it is better to work in harmony with it. But some Eastern philosophers tell us we should find enlightenment and get off the wheel altogether.

The twenty-first letter in the ancient alphabet is "Shin." Shin is the symbol of a wild, uncontrollable arrow—an arrow in jerky and wavering flight. This arrow, however, is *destined* to strike

JUDGEMENT.

somewhere, and for that reason symbolizes our ultimate fate, our "luck." This picture-letter is not coupled with an astrological sign or planet. Instead, it is conjoined with the element fire.

Twenty-two • JUDGMENT

Here, we view the scene of the Final Judgment as depicted in the Bible. One or more angels appear in the sky, and a great trumpet is sounded. The dead rise up from their sleep below.

The impressive version illustrated here is from the Rider Pack designed by Arthur Edward Waite and Pamela Colman Smith.

An important part of this card's symbolism is the sign of the cross. The cross has been used on almost every version of Judgment that has been made for the past five hundred years or so. The symbol of the cross, as depicted on the flag here, was used in the ancient Near East as a symbol of divine judgment. It separated those who were good from those who were evil.

The sign of the cross was also the glyph for the last letter in almost all of the ancient Near Eastern alphabets, including the Egyptian, the Phoenician, and the Hebrew script. Here, the letter helps to symbolize the last of the major Tarot cards.

Cardreader's Meanings. When the card of Judgment falls upright and well placed in a fortune-teller's layout, it signifies great joy because of a life well lived—joy in old age. It can also betoken the final outcome of one's life: awakening, renewal, beautifully balanced judgment, spiritual and philosophical consciousness, regeneration of mind and body after a period of suffering, the satisfactory accomplishment of work well done, a final triumph or a final judgment.

When the card falls reversed, the meanings are reversed also: shame about one's life, fear of death, fear of final justice, lack of interest in the spiritual or philosophical, unhappy old age, guilt, lack of judgment, punishment for wrongdoing, and reproach for wasted opportunities are a few of these meanings.

Philosophical Meanings. The card of Judgment acts as the balancing element—the synthesizer—of our present triad; it combines and controls the powerful forces of indeterminism (The World) and determinism (The Wheel of Fortune) with a firm, judgmental hand. It tells us there is no absolute freedom, but there is no absolute fate. The reality of our down-to-earth and mortal lives must exist somewhere in between. It is *we* who control the quality and texture of our lives because of our talent for reason, judgment, and imagination. We don't deny certain "fated" or determined elements in our universe—after all, the stars will shine tonight whether we want them to. We, instead, learn to live in harmony with the great perpetual "wheel" of determined fate. It is our judgment in these matters, our ability to step back and take a wider view, our reason and imagination, that will decide whether we will succeed or fail.

It has been said that this card, like The Moon, symbolizes the spiritual power that pulls us ahead on the long, difficult path of evolutionary progress: "the divine attraction." Judgment signifies that powerful attraction *to our source,* for Judgment represents that unknowable Creator that absorbs its own expressions back into itself.

The last letter in the ancient pictorial script is "Tau." Tau is the picture-letter that symbolizes the sign of the cross—the mark of salvation. It is the very symbol of judgment. When used as a spoken word, the letter means sign, cross, or mark.

It is known that almost all the alphabets used in the ancient

Near East used the sign of the cross as the final letter. Some of these alphabets are the ancient Hebrew, the Aramaic, the Phoenician, and the South Arabian. This special sign was also the glyph for the final letter in the Egyptian hieroglyphical script, and it was called there *the Tav cross*. And it is known that the Egyptians dedicated this letter to Thoth, the god of writing and judgment— the same Thoth who would be later transformed into the Greek's Hermes, the messenger of the gods.

The final letter is coupled with Saturn. As the *Book of Creation* relates:

> He enthroned the letter Tau in peace,
> placed a crown upon it, and combined it with the others.
> He created with them Saturn in the universe,
> the seventh day in the year, and the mouth
> of the male and female person.

Saturn is the planet that signifies self-discipline and the knowledge of responsibility. According to Greek mythology, Saturn ate his own children. In doing this, he symbolically represented that being who absorbs his own expressions back into himself. Saturn is the *teacher planet*, the planet of philosophy, profundity, and weight. He represents the urge to caution, and is the advocator of justice that is enforced with a firm hand; yet he is always fair and impartial. He is connected with such things as intense seriousness, order, conservation, realism, asceticism, and strict law. In fact, over four thousand years ago, the ancient Sumerian people called Saturn "the star of law and order" in one of their epic poems.

The card called Judgment is the twenty-second and last icon contained in the major Tarot design. It completes and fulfills that which was put into motion by The Magician (symbol of creation). It clearly informs us that the entire pictorial design was created to teach us and to enlighten us. In this way, the Tarot makes all of those who try to understand it "initiates" to a secret, sacred, and ancient mystery.

QUICK REFERENCE FOR THE MAJOR CARDS

1. The Magician: a male figure, spirited, creative, independent.
2. The High Priestess: a female figure, receptive, enlightened, wise.
3. The Empress: birth, fertility—a sensuous young person.
4. The Hierophant: inspiration, morals, religion, brotherhood, teacher.
5. The Emperor: authority, leadership, government, father.
6. The Lovers: love, attraction, aesthetics, choice.
7. The Chariot: victory and triumph with justice.
8. Strength: courage, peace, faith, domesticity.
9. The Hermit: mystical power with prudence, spiritual teacher.
10. The Fool: the seeker is especially loved by God.
11. The Sun: security, vitality, joy, lucky marriage.
12. Justice: balance, law, equity.
13. The Star: hope, purification, gifts of the spirit.
14. The Hanged Man: sacrifice, trials, idealism.
15. The Tower: catastrophe, overthrow, ruin.
16. The Devil: bondage to material things.
17. Temperance: time, moderation, communication.
18. Death: mortality, change, rebirth.
19. The Moon: anxiety, unforeseen perils, evolution.
20. The World: freedom to change, assured success.
21. The Wheel of Fortune: fate, fortune, destiny.
22. Judgment: awakening, renewal, joy in old age.

When the cards are upside down, the meanings are either weakened or opposite that listed above.

5

Reading the Tarot Cards: Some Preliminary Thoughts, Rules, and Customs

Among writers on the Tarot, there has been a good deal of speculation about the original use of these symbols. Some say the twenty-two major cards represented stages or grades used in an ancient system of initiation into the mysteries. Others say the symbols made up a "philosophical machine," a device that could answer any question and speak—by means of symbols—in all languages. And still others maintain that the Tarot was actually the master system which energized all of ancient symbolic magic; that it was the backbone of astrology, numerology, alchemy, and all of the other Hermetic sciences.

From what we have learned in the twenty-two treatments on the meanings and symbolism of the major cards, and the fifty-six treatments on the minor cards, it has become fairly clear that the Tarot could have been used for any and all of the ancient disciplines mentioned above. What is even clearer, however, is that Tarot was almost certainly used as a device to divine, and perhaps even control, the future. The use of a symbolic design like Tarot for purposes of divination, consultation, and magic was absolutely characteristic of the culture and the times we have been considering.

We also know that the ancient Egyptians used symbolic pictures, not astrology, for fortune-telling. References to some of the magical procedures are described in the surviving texts and drawings. What we cannot *prove*, though, is that these pictorial symbols resembled our Tarot pack. The pictorial sets used have not survived the ages, and there is no ancient written document that precisely describes a set of Tarot symbols.

The earliest *written document* that gives us evidence of a fortune-telling application for the cards comes to us from the mid-sixteenth century, from a book published in Venice in 1540 and titled *Le Sorti*, a work by Marcolino da Forli. The book teaches a manner of forming combinations of cards in order to divine the future. As far as we know, it is the oldest surviving book on fortune-telling with cards.

Tradition insists, however, that the art of cardreading (fortune-telling, divination, cartomancy) is much older than purely physical evidence demonstrates. According to the traditional stories, Gypsies have had the Tarot in their possession not for four or five centuries, but about fifteen centuries. When they entered Western Europe at around 1375, they were already fully initiated in the ancient art of Tarot divination; they were already masters of the reading methods I will now describe.

CARE OF THE CARDS

The serious cardreader will take steps to protect the Tarot pack as much as possible. The cards are kept carefully wrapped in a colorful piece of silk that is about the size of a large handkerchief. They are then placed in a wooden box which fits the wrapped pack snugly when it is not in use. Most readers prefer the use of a box made from *cedar,* because of its pleasant aroma. The traditional practice of protecting the pack in the manner described is, for one thing, a symbol of respect; and for another, an attempt to keep bad influences away from the cards.

Gypsy readers have the custom of keeping the wrapped cards hidden away on the top of a mantelpiece or other high, safe place whenever possible. Some Romany readers store the pack in a hidden spot in a small, protected shrine-like area where three moderate-size statues of the Blessed Virgin are displayed. This practice attests to the Gypsies' great regard for the Tarot pack combined with their great regard for the beloved "Three Marys of the Sea," the three sisters who fled the Holy Land with the Gypsy patron saint, Sara, so many years ago.

When economics or living conditions render this practice impossible, Gypsies will still insist on keeping the wrapped pack in close proximity to a statue or symbol of Our Lady, regardless of its quality or size.

In any event, the Tarot is always treated with the highest respect among the Romanys. No outsider is allowed to handle the cards unless he is a seeker involved in an actual reading. In fact, some fortune-tellers only allow the seeker to lay his hands upon the pack while he concentrates on his questions. Many times, the seeker is simply asked to pick a number of cards out of the pack and then to hand them quickly back to the diviner.

In traditional circles, it is claimed that a gifted reader builds up a kind of rapport with the energies in his or her Tarot set. Every effort is made to use the set for high and constructive purposes. Every positive event that takes place because of a good reading *adds* to the total capacity of the pack to provide further enlightenment and guidance. For this reason, a truly serious reader will take care to protect the cards and keep them as safe as possible from undesirable influences.

Serious readers are also very particular about cleanliness. The cards are laid out on a clean, clear table or other flat surface like a rug, a grassy area, or a spot on a clean floor. Sometimes these larger areas are helpful. They are uncluttered, and some readings take up a moderate to large amount of space.

The hands of both the diviner and the seeker should be clean and free of any oily substance. Oil can quickly ruin a perfectly good set of Tarot cards.

SETTING THE RIGHT MOOD

Good cardreaders strive for a friendly, comfortable, and peaceful atmosphere while meditating on their Tarot. Both the seeker and the reader should feel free to relax and concentrate on the reading as much as possible; and the use of dimmed lighting, pleasant soft music, and some incense is usually quite helpful in this respect. Loud noise, constant interruptions, and observers who are boisterous and talkative should be avoided whenever possible.

Tarot reading is a constructive and supportive discipline, and it is certainly not the intention of a good reader to shock or frighten the seeker. Gypsy tradition insists that subjects regarding death and disaster are almost never brought up in a reading; in fact, with the uninitiated, this practice is strictly forbidden.

There are a number of cards in the pack that can be interpreted in a dismal and unpleasant fashion. Most of the time, however, these cards are read as optimistically as possible. The best readers know that it takes years of experience and a great deal of talent with the symbolism before any reader can handle some of the more difficult and negative cards found in the system. It helps to remember that all Tarot symbols must be read in relation to other symbolic placements in the layout. For this reason, the art of reading "bad cards" is a very delicate procedure that takes a good deal of fine judgment and a good deal of experience with actual reading situations.

Tarot reading is a responsibility. It should be remembered that most people could be upset by an insensitive reading—or even worse, a dismal one. It is far better to give sound advice based on the wisdom contained in the cards than to jolt someone with that brand of stark reality that concentrates on pain and sorrow in people's lives. This is not to say, however, that a reader just tells the seeker exactly what he wants to hear—sugarcoats the message. Readers, at times, will give stern and penetrating interpretations and will not hold back on the harder negative meanings; but this is done with a strong element of consideration, and done with people who are known to be able to handle it.

Tarot reading, like almost everything else, comes down to a matter of practice, talent, and *experience*. Eden Gray has reminded us that all readings contain an element of uncertainty; that it is not a good idea to say absolutely that an event will happen; and that it is better to say that the event appears very probable, considering the current course of events. The major Tarot card called The World teaches us that part of the future is in the hands of the individual and that everything is subject to change.

In fortune-telling, simplicity and straightforwardness tend to work best. Long-winded or highly philosophical expositions on the meaning of each card will detract from the overall effect. If a certain card is not understood, or seems to make no sense in a particular position, it should be passed over. The strong, meaningful, positive cards, on the other hand, should be given preference.

It helps very much to become as familiar as possible with the meanings of all the cards. This can be mastered by constantly rereading the sections on "primary meanings" given in this book. It also helps to remember that working with the Tarot is a matter of understanding and not just of memory. The minor Tarot, for example, can be mastered by remembering what the four suits mean symbolically and by taking the meanings of the first ten numbers into consideration. This method is much more rewarding, and much easier, than rote memorization.

One way to improve your confidence, your reading skill, and your familiarity with the cards is to do hypothetical readings for a nonexistent seeker. These practice readings can make you a lot more sure of yourself and greatly improve your concentration. Do not, however, try to actually read the Tarot cards for yourself—divine your own future. Most Gypsy instructors forbid self-readings. They are known not to work correctly.

CHOOSING A SIGNIFICATOR

At the beginning of a Tarot reading, even before the cards are shuffled, the fortune-teller will search through the pack and find one special card that best describes the characteristics of the seeker. This special card is called "the significator." It is always chosen from among the picture cards in the minor Tarot—one of the Kings, Queens, Knights, or Pages—and it is placed in the middle of the cardreader's table.

The significator is chosen on the basis of the seeker's age, sex, complexion, general physical characteristics, and the intuitive feeling that the reader "picks up" from the individual. If the seeker is already known by the reader, then of course his or her personality characteristics will play a more important part in the determination of the best significator.

Male seekers who are around 25 years of age or older will have one of the picture cards called "Kings" chosen for them. Female seekers over the age of 20 or so (or mothers of children) will have one of the Queens chosen. Teenagers and young adults of *either sex* will have one of the Knights chosen. And smaller children of either sex will be signified by one of the Pages.

The suit marking of the particular card chosen depends, of course, on the complexion, physical type, and personality traits (when known) of the individual seeker. In general, Wands represent tanned, healthy-looking, and spirited people from the working class. Cups represent gentle, moderately built, and primarily artistic people from the class of teachers, healers, creators, and poets. Swords represent active, busy, primarily intellectual personalities who have what can be called a city person's aura and who are from the class of rule, decision, and command. And Pentacles represent solid-looking, down-to-earth people who are usually connected with business, trade, or security. They will, many times, have either a very light or a very dark complexion.

The choice of the correct significator is rather relaxed and subjective, and a good deal depends on the judgment of the reader. It is easy enough, for example, to find the correct significator for a 30-year-old woman who is an artist, who appears primarily emotional, and who has a medium complexion. She would of course be signified by the Queen of Cups. It would also be easy to find the significator for a young man in his early twenties who is a city person, primarily intellectual, and a law student. He would certainly be a Knight of Swords. But what of a businessman who loves poetry, or a primarily intellectual and commanding woman who has a healthy, tanned complexion? With these types, a good deal of judgment and intuition must come into play so that the right suit is chosen. With experience, one will learn to place much more trust in one's *feelings* about a particular seeker than on surface matters such as complexion. Common sense tells us that not all earthy people have extreme coloring and not all intellectuals have pale, city-person complexions.

Most people enjoy having their significator chosen. It is, after all, the symbol that represents *them* in the reading. Finding the significator helps to break the ice, in a sense. It allows both reader and seeker to know each other a little better. And it allows the seeker an opportunity to view many (if not all) of the symbols on the cards as the reader searches through them for just the right one.

Once the significator is found and placed in the middle of the reader's table, it is time to find out whether the seeker has a specific question or questions that he would like answered in the session. Questions the seeker might have can be helpful, but they are not necessary. Sometimes the seeker may want a general reading, and in that case there may be no question.

I have noticed that many readings not only answer any questions posed by the individual, but also go deeper than that— to the root of the question, the source of the problem or concern. The quality of any reading, however, depends on the amount of energy put into it by both the seeker and the reader. It is important to let the seeker know from the beginning that the level of the reading will depend a good deal on his ability to concentrate and to focus his energy into the cards. One can only get from the Tarot what he puts into it.

There are different reading methods or layouts used by traditional fortune-tellers. Some take a short time. Some take much longer. Some are quite serious; others are lighter and more entertaining. The ones I present here were chosen because they work best. In a sense, they are the classics.

6

Various Cardreading Methods

THE OLD KELTIC METHOD

No one knows exactly how old the Keltic method of reading Tarot cards really is, but it is certainly the most popular and most widely used of all the reading methods known today. It is very popular because it works well for beginners, it is a relatively simple method (only ten cards and a significator are used), and at the same time it is a very revealing and powerful method. It yields intense, striking, and interesting symbolic messages in a clear and straightforward manner.

Although there are no written records to prove it, Romany tradition tells us that Gypsies brought this "Keltic" method into England and Ireland with them in the fifteenth century. It is known the Gypsies were harshly persecuted in these lands at that time because of their "outrageous and naughty practices," not the least of which was fortune-telling.

It is also known that the layout itself shows numerological and symbolic designs that are both ancient and profound.

The first step in this method, as with most others, is to pick out a good significator (pages 144–146). While this is being done, the seeker may of course get a full view of all the Tarot

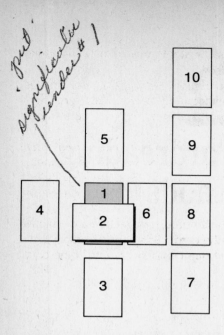

put 'significator' in number # 1

The Oswald Wirth Tarot laid out in a top view of
the old Keltic configuration.

symbols; and for this reason it is a good time for you to become
more familiar with and to answer any questions of the seeker.
The significator should be that one special picture card that best
describes the outward personality and physical characteristics of
the seeker. Once the significator is found, it should be placed in
the middle of a clean, clear reading surface.

Ask the seeker to get comfortable, and give him the remainder
of the Tarot pack so that he can shuffle it. Many times, it helps
to have the seeker sit on the same side of the reading table as
the reader. That way, the seeker can view the layout from the
front also.

Explain to the seeker that the pack you have just handed him
has all of its cards right side up; that you have turned all of them
upright in preparation for the reading. Also explain that "reversals," cards that fall upside down in a reading, can have negative
or weak meanings. Because of this, he must keep a sense, while
shuffling, of which end of the pack is the top. He must not turn

any cards upside down unless he wants them that way—unless he feels they should be reversed.

It is best for the seeker to shuffle the cards in the simplest manner. Fancier shuffling methods will accidentally turn many of the cards upside down, and the seeker may not be aware of this.

If the seeker has a question, he should concentrate on it while he shuffles the cards. It is not necessary for the person being read for to make the question known to the reader. They can keep the question private if they so desire. Many times, the subject of a reading will have no questions.

The seeker should relax, concentrate, and get into a meditative state of mind while shuffling the cards. It is at this point that you should remind the person that one can only get out of the cards what one puts into them.

The seeker should continue to shuffle until he feels that the cards are "right," that is, in an order that feels perfect. Once this is accomplished, ask him to hand you the pack in its upright position.

The reader seldom reshuffles the cards after they have been designated "right" by the seeker. There are instances, however, where a reader will feel dissatisfied with the condition of the pack and may shuffle them further.

The top ten cards are now dealt in accord with the design shown here. Each position in this design has a special meaning, and these meanings are as follows.

Card number one: *The Covering Card*. This card is placed on top of the significator so that it covers it almost completely. The Covering Card represents the general atmosphere or aura that surrounds the reading. It can signify the basis of the seeker's question or problem, the subconscious motivation behind the question, the foundation of the personality, or the seeker's concern at its most basic level. As you place this card on the reading table, say aloud, "This card covers you."

Card number two: *The Crossing Card*. The second card is laid across the first one as illustrated. The Crossing Card is always read as an upright symbol. It is never read as reversed. The symbol that falls into this position represents forces that can work either *for* or *against* the seeker. It is up to the reader to decide whether the card that falls here is helpful. As you place

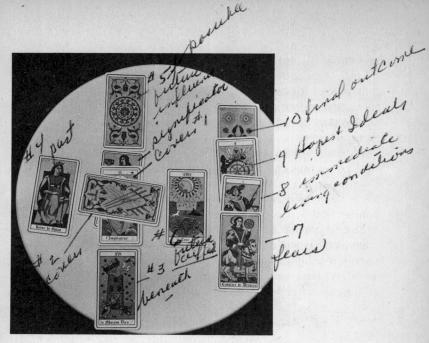

Handwritten annotations around the image:

#5 future possible picture influence

signuficator covers #1

#6 past

10 final outcome

9 Hopes Ideals

8 immediate living conditions

7 fears

#2 covers

#3 picture verified beneath

Layout for the Keltic method of fortune-telling.

the card on the others, say aloud, "This card crosses you."

Card number three: *The Foundation Card.* The third Tarot symbol drawn from the pack is placed beneath the first group just as illustrated. It represents something that has become a strong part of the seeker's most deeply rooted experience, something that characterizes his or her personality. It helps us clarify and bring to light the seeker's real concerns and questions. In a sense, it mirrors the foundations of the person's psyche. Place this card at the base of the reading and say aloud, "This card goes beneath you."

Card number four: *The Card of the Past.* The fourth card drawn from the pack is one of the most important. It is usually of great interest to the seeker. The card represents a crucial past event in the person's life—an unforgettable experience. The effect of this experience was very strong at the time, but its further effects are getting weaker and weaker as time goes by. Perhaps in the future it will be almost totally forgotten. The card is placed at the left of the design as shown, and the reader then says aloud, "This card goes behind you."

Card number five: *The Card of Future Influences*. The fifth card placed in the Tarot reading signifies possible future influences: things that *may* take place in the future. Picture cards in this position almost always represent people. Other cards can represent events, psychological influences, or similar forces. Place this card at the top of the design and say aloud, "This card goes above you."

Card number six: *The Card of the Future*. The sixth symbol placed in the Keltic design tells us of definite future events or of definite future influences. This card must be read carefully because here we are entering the realm of true fortune-telling. Experience with the symbolism on the cards and good concentration will help a good deal, but the best at this art have a special talent. Place the sixth card on the right, as illustrated, and say aloud, "This card goes before you."

Card number seven: *The Card of Fears*. The seventh card drawn from the pack represents something the seeker is afraid of. This "thing" can be a person, an event, or even a concept. Many times the card of fears is somehow connected with the person's question—his concern expressed to the reader in the first place. The position not only represents fears, but also worries and anxiety in general. The card is placed in the seventh position as shown and the reader says aloud, "These are your fears."

Card number eight: *The Card of the House*. This card describes the immediate living conditions of the seeker: his family, his friends, and the quality of his environment. In fact, the card mainly describes the surroundings, the environment of the person being read for. If, for example, a Three of Cups should fall into this position, that would be interpreted as a very good sign, an indication that the seeker came from a friendly, cooperative, and very loving home life, a home that should yield a great deal of happiness.

The card is placed in the design as shown, and the reader then says, "This is your house."

Card number nine: *The Card of Hopes and Ideals*. The ninth symbol drawn from the Tarot pack represents the hopes and ideals of the seeker. Many times the hopes and aspirations signified here have something to do with the seeker's question.

Other times, however, they will just be broad and general. This card is placed in the ninth position, and the reader says, "These are your hopes."

Card number ten: *The Card of the Final Outcome.* The tenth card is the last symbol drawn in the Keltic method. It is most likely the most difficult position for any reader to interpret because it signifies the final outcome of a matter related directly to the seeker's question. It will help to remember that this symbol is influenced and modified by the other nine cards appearing in the layout. The whole layout should be examined before an attempt is made to give the true meaning of this particular card.

This symbol is placed in the tenth position, as shown, and the reader says aloud, "This is the final outcome."

Once all of the ten cards, and the significator, are laid out according to the design, the reader should consider all of them carefully before coming to any conclusions. In general, the cards are explained in the same order they were laid out in: the covering card is spoken of first, then the crossing card, and so on. Sometimes deviation from this natural order may work better for some reason, and it's perfectly all right to let the reading flow in a more random style, especially after some experience has been gained with reading the symbols.

It takes quite a bit of intuition, practice, and imagination in order to be accurate and convincing as a Tarot reader. With the Keltic method, as with most others, one must read the symbolism on the cards; but one must also fully understand what each of the ten positions stands for symbolically.

There is no reason to be discouraged if at first your readings are a bit slow and self-conscious. Mastering the Tarot takes time and practice. It helps, of course, to constantly review the information on primary fortune-teller's meanings covered earlier. It also helps to do some practice readings once in a while. Familiarity with the deeper symbolism connected with the major Tarot cards, provided here, is also helpful. Note also that the fortune-teller's information was provided in a short listing. This should make quick reference easier.

The Keltic method is ideal for most beginners because it is clear and strong in presentation. Also, it does not consume a great deal of time. The average time is thirty minutes to one hour. Longer readings can be exhausting to both the seeker and the reader. And shorter Tarot readings don't always have the same effect and power.

When reading cards with the Keltic method, and with all other methods, for that matter, it helps to remember that major Tarot cards are a good deal more powerful than the minor cards. They usually contain a good deal more seriousness and impact.

THE TWENTY-ONE-CARD GYPSY METHOD

This method is the most widely used among the more old-fashioned and traditional of the Romany fortune-tellers. Despite the large number of cards used, the method is almost as easy and fast-moving as the Keltic.

Twenty-one cards are laid out as seven sets of triads with the significator crowning them at the exact physical center. In this respect, the design conforms to one of the most ancient of symbolic plans. Constructions like this were used by Egyptians, Hebrews, and others thousands of years ago; and the seven sets of triads have always been regarded as one of the most magical of all the numerological forms. The cardreading Gypsies have preserved for us a style of symbolic expression here that could be well over four thousand years old, but they speak very little of its deeper secrets.

To begin this reading, have the seeker seat himself so that he can clearly view all of the reading area from the same vantage as the reader.

Pick out the significator in the usual manner.

Place the significator in the center of the reading area, and have the seeker shuffle the Tarot cards as usual.

The subject of the reading should concentrate as he shuffles the cards. If he has a question, he should ask it while shuffling. Remember to remind the seeker to keep a sense of the right-side-up end of the pack. No reversals should be made by accident.

When the seeker feels that the cards have been shuffled into their correct order, they are handed back to the reader in their right-side-up position.

Now fan out all of the cards before the seeker and ask him to pick out twenty-one cards, carefully and one at a time. The pack should be facedown so the seeker can't see the cards he is choosing. Once the twenty-one cards are chosen, the remaining ones should be set aside.

Place the cards in the design exactly in accord with the numerical order illustrated below. Note that the triads do not have to form triangles. Sometimes this takes up too much space. They can be placed in straight lines of three cards each, as shown here.

The Significator						
A	B	C	D	E	F	G
1	2	3	4	5	6	7
8	9	10	11	12	13	14
15	16	17	18	19	20	21

Each triad can now be read as one symbolic "house," and the individual meanings of these triads are as follows.

Triad A: This house defines the seeker's present psychological outlook.

Triad B: These three cards describe the seeker's present home life, or his environment in general.

Triad C: This triad signifies the seeker's hopes, desires, and aspirations, many times related to his question.

Triad D: This house describes the seeker's strong points, his symbols of good luck. It is a friendly triad.

Triad E: These cards describe the seeker's weak points, the things he must be warned of. This is the triad of severity and power.

Triad F: This triad predicts the seeker's immediate future. It can also betoken definite future influences.

Triad G: And this triad predicts the long-term outcome of the matter at hand. It is similar to the Keltic *Card of the Final Outcome.*

The triads are read in alphabetical order from left to right. The cards in each triad are read as positive (the top card); negative (the middle card); and neutralizing (the bottom card) principles, just as we noticed when we examined the major Tarot design.

Because of this, the reader can gain very rich messages from this method.

The Gypsy method of reading should be taken just a bit more slowly than the Keltic method. Each triad should be considered carefully until the combination of symbols makes clear sense to the reader. Rich and powerful indications should be expected, especially if both parties to the reading are concentrating well. The combination of symbols in a given triad can many times be very striking. It is possible, for example, that three cards of the same suit may show up in a particular triad; and this, as you learned earlier, is a powerful indication. It is even possible that three cards from the *major tarot* may show up in the same triad—and that, of course, is a very powerful indication.

The best-kept secret regarding this method is that the three cards in each triad are viewed as positive principle (thesis), negative principle (antithesis), and neutral principle (synthesis) while they are being examined by the reader. The method has been used by non-Gypsies for years, but never in the exactly correct manner. No book that I know of has given the complete instructions.

The twenty-one-card Gypsy reading can be slightly more time-consuming and slightly more complex than the old Keltic method, but the color and the resonance of the symbolic messages it sometimes expresses certainly make the extra effect worth it. A typical reading usually takes from forty-five minutes to an hour, but some readings can take even longer.

It is a good idea to set aside quite a bit of free space on the reading area before attempting to use this design. Most Tarot packs are larger than the common playing cards we are used to.

THE SINGLE TRIAD METHOD

The reader picks three cards. The first is the card of the past. It is read in a style similar to that used in the Keltic method: as a symbol of an important past event that is fading in energy as time goes by.

The card of the present is read next. It describes an important person, event, or preoccupation that is part of the seeker's present life.

The card of the future is read last. It is read in a manner similar to the Card of the Final Outcome in the Keltic method. Remember, there is usually a much lighter mood about this style of reading.

An experienced cardreader can do around eight to ten of these simple readings in somewhat over an hour, but of course they lose the depth of the other more serious methods because of their speed.

The single triad method can be used for serious readings if it is slowed down a good deal. The depth of any Tarot reading depends on the amount of time and concentration put into it, not so much the *style* of reading used.

THE NEW YEAR'S EVE READING

The New Year's Eve reading method is usually done during the festive week preceding the new year. The favorite time for this is on New Year's Eve itself. Like the single triad method, this style of reading can be done in a graceful, fast-moving, and lighthearted manner, and it always gives a great deal of enjoyment at social gatherings.

The object of the reading is to give the seeker information about the most important event, meeting, or change that will take place within each season of the following year. There are only four cards used, plus a significator.

The significator is chosen and the cards are shuffled by the seeker in the usual way. The person need not worry about the upright condition of the cards, because there are no reversals used with this method. All cards are dealt right side up.

Once the cards are shuffled, the reader takes them, fans them out before the seeker, and asks that he carefully pick out four of them. The cards should be held so the seeker cannot see their symbols. The four cards are placed in the design as illustrated below.

SPRING		SUMMER
	SIGNIFICATOR	
FALL		WINTER

The first card the seeker hands you represents an important event in spring. The second card, summer—and so on.

Cards from the suit of Wands are regarded as very powerful in the "spring" position because the symbol of the Wand represents springtime. Cards from the suit of Cups find extra energy in the "summer" position. Pentacles find their greatest strength in the "fall" position. Swords are most powerful in the "winter" position. The major Tarot cards are, of course, very powerful when found anywhere.

Although the New Year's method described here is the most popular, two simple variations are sometimes used. In some instances, twelve cards are chosen instead of four. These twelve cards are used to represent an important energy covering each *month* of the coming year. This method, however, takes up more time.

In other instances, the reading will take place on or near the seeker's birthday. When this is the case, the four cards will represent the four upcoming seasons, or the twelve cards will represent the twelve months coming after the particular birthday.

These reading methods are usually done in a lighthearted style. They lend themselves to parties and social gatherings where the object of using the cards is mostly fun. Don't be fooled, however, into thinking this style of reading is easy. It takes a good deal of talent to read these symbols quickly, confidently, and accurately. This is especially true when one wants to keep the readings on the light side.

The average time taken for the four-card method is about fifteen minutes. The twelve-card method can take around an hour.

AN ESOTERIC GYPSY METHOD

The design used here is similar to that used in the twenty-one-card Gypsy method described earlier: Seven sets of triads are laid out on the reading table and they are crowned by a significator. The difference is, the cards are placed in a different numerical order, and each of the twenty-one positions has its own special significance.

Because twenty-one separate positions have to be read, the method is time-consuming and complex. Therefore it should only be used by those who have a good deal of experience with the cards. It is a serious method of cardreading, and it speaks of events from the seeker's entire life. It then projects directly into the events of the future.

The design used in this method is illustrated on page 159. It should be somewhat familiar to the reader because it has a surface similarity to that used in the twenty-one-card Gypsy method. The cards can be laid out as seven sets of triangles as shown here, or they can be compressed into straight lines as with the earlier diagram in order to save space on the reading table.

First, a significator is chosen and placed in the upper center of a large, clear reading space. Second, the reader shuffles the entire pack—except of course for the significator—until she feels they are in good order. And third, the reader hands the pack to the seeker and asks the person to feel through it so that he might pick out twenty-one cards that appeal to him. The seeker may spread the cards facedown to accomplish this.

Once the twenty-one cards are chosen and removed from the whole deck, the remainder of the pack is set aside.

These twenty-one cards are now shuffled by the seeker until he "feels" they are in the right order. When this is done, the reader takes the cards in their right-side-up condition and places them on the reading table in the exact numerical sequence illustrated. (A few cards may be reversed and they should be allowed to remain so.)

Each of the twenty-one positions has a special symbolic meaning.

Card Number One: *The Father's Card.* The first position

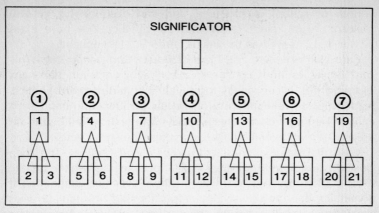

This illustration represents a typical Gypsy-style fortune-telling layout. Here we find twenty-one Tarot cards laid out as a set of seven triangles with one special card crowning the design at the top of the fourth triangle. One special figure (in this case, the significator) remains alone at the center.

contains a card that describes the seeker's father or some other early male figure who had a determining influence. In general, the card will describe some characteristic of a powerful male influence in childhood. If the symbol called "The Magician" falls here, that is considered to be a very intense indication, as he is one of the ultimate father figures.

Card Number Two: *The Mother's Card.* This position describes some characteristic of the seeker's mother or some other important female figure in childhood. The card falling here can describe her position in life, her wishes, her qualities, her attitudes, or her talents. A High Priestess placed here denotes a very highly evolved female figure.

Card Number Three: *The Card of the Child.* The third position describes the seeker as a younger person or child. It may represent his personality, his desires, his experiences, or his environment. All minor cards with the number three on them are considered to be extra-powerful here. The Empress finds her greatest energy here.

Card Number Four: *The Card of Teachings and Beliefs.* This represents an element of the seeker's moral, ethical, or religious training, probably in his early years. It recounts his formative church or school experiences, and can describe his general philosophy. All minor cards with the number four have extra power here, as well as the major card, The Hierophant.

Card Number Five: *The Card of Power and Leadership*. This position represents a coming of age: dealing with the challenges of this world. It can signify the seeker's attitude toward politics, leadership, power, and control. In this position the major card called The Emperor denotes a seeker with high aptitude in these areas. The symbol called The Sun is also powerful here.

Card Number Six: *The Card of Taste and Choices*. The sixth position describes the things that appeal to the seeker on the artistic or sensual level. The position specifies someone or something that the seeker finds appealing and beautiful. Gypsies many times use it to signify the seeker's first great love. For a man, the appearance of The High Priestess in this place denotes an important love affair in the present or future.

Card Number Seven: *The Card of Movement and Conflict*. This position defines things having to do with travel, military experiences, new discoveries, and great conflicts that are usually intellectual. It can describe the seeker's attitude toward these things or his innate mental capabilities. Cards in the suit of Swords are strong here, and so are the major Tarots called The Chariot and Temperance.

Card Number Eight: *The Card of the Home and Possessions*. The eighth position describes the domestic life of the seeker: his home and family life in the past, present, or future. Sometimes the position describes the seeker's attitude about these things. The card called Strength is most powerful in this location.

Card Number Nine: *The Card of Prudence and Protection*. This position describes an area where the seeker should listen to wise counsel and take caution. Sometimes the card describes the person who will give counsel, protection, or enlightenment. The major Tarots called "The Fool" and "The Hermit" are known to have special power here.

Card Number Ten: *The Card of Well-Being and Security*. The tenth position describes something that gives the seeker a strong sense of contentment and security. It denotes a force that preserves and protects him. Bad or unpleasantly reversed cards are weak here. Positive, happy cards—especially The Fool and The Sun—are known to be most powerful in this location. Picture cards falling here usually describe people who bring a great deal of happiness to the seeker.

Card Number Eleven: *The Card of the Law*. This position will represent the seeker's attitudes regarding justice and the law. It can also represent the outcome of some legal dispute. The major Tarot cards called Judgment and Justice are known to be strong here, and so are all minor Tarot cards marked with a two.

Card Number Twelve: *The Card of Hope, Luck, and Imagination*. This position denotes something that the seeker will have very good luck with, something that is the product of his hopeful imagination, something that is wished for. Strong happy cards signify that these dreams will come true. Bad cards are severely weakened in this location and no card is reversed.

Card Number Thirteen: *The Card of Sacrifice and Discipline*. The thirteenth position describes something that the seeker is willing to fight and sacrifice for. The position reveals the source of the person's ethical courage. Sometimes this source may be a person. Other times it may be an ideal. Among minor cards, the fives are usually bad cards, but not so in this location. Instead, their most positive aspects are amplified.

Card Number Fourteen: *The Card of Disaster*. The fourteenth position signifies something that the seeker should be very cautious about unless he is prepared for severe circumstances. Most cards are not well placed here. Bad cards are even worse. The major cards called Temperance and The World tame down this position.

Card Number Fifteen: *The Card of Bondage*. This position pertains to things that keep the seeker stifled and tied down—powers that keep him bonded to material objects and material problems. Good cards are badly placed in this location, and both The Hierophant and The Devil have great energy.

Card Number Sixteen: *The Card of Communication*. The sixteenth position describes the talents and preferences of the seeker regarding all forms of communication. Some will reach other people through art, others through material things, and still others through intellect, intuition, or even conflict. There are an infinite number of variations describing an infinite number of personalities. The cards called Temperance and The Chariot are strong here.

Card Number Seventeen: *The Card of Changes*. This position

can describe three different possibilities regarding the subject of change. Most times, it signifies a drastic change that will occur in the near future. At other times it will symbolize a limit that cannot be overcome until an important change is made. In still other instances the card falling here can describe the seeker's attitude to change in general. Both The Magician and the card called Temperance are known to have strong energies here.

Card Number Eighteen: *The Card of Fears and Anxieties*. The eighteenth position describes things or relationships that the seeker fears. These things have given him worry and anxiety over a long period of time. Once the fears are overcome, the seeker will make great progress. The cards called The Moon and The Empress are quite powerful in this position, and the appearance of the card of Temperance indicates that the seeker has little to be concerned about.

Card Number Nineteen: *The Card of Hopes and Aspirations*. This position serves the function identical to that used in the Keltic method. It describes the seeker's hopes for the future and sometimes portrays actual events that may take place. Picture cards almost always represent people who will be helpful. The card called Strength has extra energy here.

Card Number Twenty: *The Card of Fate*. The card falling in the twentieth position signifies something that will happen in the future: a definite future influence, a person, or a situation. The card called "The Wheel Of Fortune" has an especially striking impact here, and is noted as a sign of good luck whether upright or reversed.

Card Number Twenty-one: *The Card of the Final Outcome*. The final card pertains to a definite outcome related to the seeker's question or to the reading in general. The symbol may describe a person, a situation, or an attitude. All cards are known to have their most positive energies about them in this, the final, position.

The esoteric Gypsy method is chronological. It covers events from the past, the present, and the future. For this reason, the age of the seeker must be considered. For a child, all positions above the seventh can be considered cards denoting future events. For a very old person, only the last three cards can be viewed as denoting the future.

Once all twenty-one cards are laid out, it is a good idea to take notice of which suit, if any, dominates the reading. If we find, for instance, that ten of the cards are from the suit of Pentacles, we should view this as an indication that money and security are the prime factors in the reading or are somehow connected with the seeker. Groups of similar cards (major cards, for example) do show up in single triads, and they can give remarkable indications when accurately read.

Weak cards—that is, cards that do not make much sense in a particular location—are simply passed by. In a normal reading, a reader may expect four or five cards to fall into this category. If more than that show up in a reading of this type, it probably means that the seeker (or the reader) is not up to full concentration. Perhaps a simpler and less demanding method should be tried.

The esoteric method will take from one to two hours to complete. The length of the reading depends, of course, on the amount of time given to each of the twenty-one cards by the reader. Some readings, because of the strength and clarity of certain Tarot symbols, will be much more substantial than others; but again, a great deal depends upon the concentration and the mood of both parties.